BALLET BASICS

BALLET BASICS

SECOND EDITION

Sandra Noll Hammond

MAYFIELD PUBLISHING COMPANY

Second edition

Library of Congress Catalog Card Number: 83-062823
International Standard Book Number: 0-87484-589-0

Manufactured in the United States of America

10 9

Mayfield Publishing Company
1240 Villa Street
Mountain View, California 94041

Sponsoring editor: C. Lansing Hays
Manuscript editor: Mary Anne Stewart
Managing editor: Pat Herbst
Art director and designer: Nancy Sears
Illustrator: Diana Thewlis
Production manager: Cathy Willkie
Compositor: Dharma Press
Printer and binder: George Banta Company

CONTENTS

PREFACE

The popular image of the beginning ballet student is that of a knobby-kneed ten-year-old girl, eyes sparkling with dreams of becoming a ballerina. This book, however, is written for the beginning ballet student who is at least eight years older than that dreamy-eyed child. For a variety of reasons this person, male or female, has enrolled in an adult beginning ballet class—at a college or university, in a department of physical education or fine arts, in a community or arts center, in a private studio or professional dancing school. No matter where the ballet class meets, certain fundamental activities and, yes, protocol will be observed. This book hopes to introduce and explain the basic outline of the ballet class—the work at the *barre* and in the center, the dress and comportment of the student, the function of the classroom itself, and the role of the teacher.

The study of ballet as a means to a career as a professional dancer is not very realistic for the adult beginner. There are a few, very rare, exceptions of talented latecomers who began the study of ballet in their late teens and later joined one company or another as professional dancers. But even those rare cases are almost always men who came to ballet after several years of training in other forms of dance (tap or jazz) or in a related activity such as gymnastics.

It is assumed, therefore, that the reader probably does not dream of becoming a professional ballet dancer. Is there a valid reason for an adult to study ballet? I believe the answer is yes and, moreover, a plural yes.

Ballet technique involves and challenges the entire body. Its intricacies and harmonies stimulate the mind as well as the muscles. For total body exercise it has few equals. The determined student even eventually may discover performing, teaching, and choreographing opportunities in the ever-multiplying amateur groups, civic or regional. Certainly new and expanded opportunities exist in ballet-related fields, for which an understanding of ballet technique is a benefit and often an actual requirement.

The execution of ballet technique can do more than exercise muscles and strengthen ligaments or provide an outlet for the performing urge. When done carefully and correctly, it can improve body posture and carriage and, eventually, the actual shape of the body. It can stimulate the appreciation of dance as a medium of expression. Admittedly, progress in these directions may be slow in an adult after years of habitual careless posture, accumulated tensions, and desultory attendance at dance concerts. For the person who would attempt to correct such habits, the ballet classroom is one place to begin, the modern dance classroom being, of course, another.

A student who has chosen the ballet classroom will soon be immersed in an art rich in four centuries of history, an art form worthy of serious study by an adult. The evolution of ballet is detalied in many fascinating books, but reading about ballet cannot begin to impart the excitement and understanding that study from a good classroom teacher can—a teacher whose expertise is part of that historical legacy. Books such as this one are offered as an aid to, not a substitute for, that study.

This revised edition contains completely new illustrations and expanded, updated material in each chapter. In addition to inclusion of some important new artists and companies emerging in the last decade, Chapter 1, "Ballet History," narrows, and thus sharpens, its focus to present a clearer background for the primary subject of this volume: ballet technique. Additional technical material for *barre* and center work and for *allegro*, as well as clarification and expansion of technical descriptions, is incorporated in Chapters 2 through 5. Chapters 6 and 7, "The Ballet Body" and "The Ballet Profession," reflect recent interest in, and understanding of, the health of dancers and the development of new opportunities for careers in ballet-related fields.

The intention of the book remains that of an auxiliary source, augmenting the beginning ballet class not only by supplying technical information but also by serving as a concise reference for a historical perspective, a technical vocabulary, the care of the dancer's instrument—the body—and an introduction to the ballet profession.

I wish to thank my ballet instructors who, through the years, have indirectly helped me write this book: Margaret Craske and Antony Tudor, The Juilliard School and the Metropolitan Opera School of Ballet; Alan Howard, Pacific Ballet, San Francisco; Thalia Mara and Arthur Mahoney, School of Ballet Repertory, New York City; Dolores Mitrovich, Tucson, Arizona; and my very first teachers, Toby Jorgensen and Sue Keller, Fayetteville, Arkansas.

I also want to thank the following reviewers for their thoughtful reading of a preliminary draft of the manuscript: Ronnie Brosterman of Scripps College, Cathy Fox of the University of Tennessee, and Barbara Plunk of the University of California at Irvine.

New illustrations for this edition were made from photographs taken by Jared M. Hammond, G. Benton Johnson, and Jovan Nikolic of dancers Norrine Bessor, Dan Dowker, Katie Gill, Rodney Gustafson, Tamara Lohrenz, Denise Rinaldi, Edward Rumberger, and Michaele Sallade. Special thanks also go to Julie McLeod and the Dance Warehouse of Santa Barbara for providing studio space for photography sessions.

S.N.H.

BALLET BASICS

CHAPTER 1
BALLET HISTORY

Ballet today is not easy to define. A typical performance may include a twenty-minute excerpt from a "classical" ballet of nineteenth-century Russia, a one-act modern ballet, and a ballet that employs a popular style such as jazz or rock. The subject matter of these selections may range from a child's fairy tale to a psychological drama to an abstract idea, or it may be a "pure dance" ballet with no subject at all. The dancers may wear "toe" shoes or "street" shoes or no shoes. Costumes may look as if they had come straight out of a king's closet in the eighteenth century or directly from a contemporary ballet studio, leg warmers and all. Indeed, sometimes costumes appear to be missing, creating the illusion, if not the reality, of nudity.

The differences in movement can be equally striking. The dancers may move in a grand, noble manner; they may appear to spend more time in the air than on the ground; they may dazzle the audience with the speed of their turns and the beats of their legs—all characteristics of classical ballet. In the next dance, however, the same performers may explore areas of expression in body movement and stage space in a manner more akin to modern dance than to ballet. Another time the movement may seemingly have wandered off the Broadway stage or out of the television screen.

Although these ballets are apparently quite dissimilar, they nevertheless are all called *ballets*—and for two important reasons: (1) They are all theatrical performances that blend planned, organized movement (choreography), music (or other sound), and decor (scenic design, lighting, costumes); and (2) they are all performed by dancers who have been trained primarily in what is called classical, or academic, ballet technique.

The development of these two characteristics—theatrical ballet performance and classical ballet technique—is the subject of this chapter, by necessity viewed here more in outline than in detail.

THE DEVELOPMENT OF WESTERN THEATRICAL DANCE

One of the intriguing questions to be asked by dance enthusiasts today of dancers of the past is, How exactly did you dance? Correlatively, ballet dancers of today may well wonder about the origins and evolution of the dance technique and style they are expected to master in today's classrooms and to perform in contemporary theatres.

Accounting for the past is not an easy task in the dance realm. Of all the arts, the art of movement is the most ephemeral—disappearing almost as it occurs, leaving few and inexact records of its brief glory. ("Ballet is now . . . now is when it happens" was a familiar saying of choreographer George Balanchine, founder and artistic director of the New York City Ballet until his death in 1983.)

In this century, technological developments in film and video tape allow a certain preservation of today's repertories that dances of earlier centuries never enjoyed. Recent respect for, but by no means universal use of, newly improved dance notation systems encourages relatively accurate preservation of contemporary choreography (see p. 153). But much of ballet's history, especially its technical and choreographic history, has been lost for lack of a generally accepted and precise recording device. Unlike students of opera, drama, or painting—who can study and practice from scores, scripts, or canvases—dance students have had to rely almost exclusively on personal contact with practitioners of their art. Exactly what did the dancing masters of the past teach their pupils? Seeking that answer has become the focus of much recent research in dance history and will be the theme of this brief survey.

A TRADITION BEGINS

The origins of ballet can be, and have been, interpreted differently. A popular notion is that it all began in Czarist Russia during the nineteenth century when some dancer put on a new kind of dance slipper and thereby rose onto toetips. A more sophisticated view traces ballet's beginnings, and certainly its heritage, to the opera-ballets and dancing schools of eighteenth-century Europe. Other interpretations point to the seventeenth-century French court ballets and academies that developed during the monarchy of Louis XIV, but which were evolving even during reigns of the previous century.

If, however, one seeks to trace the tradition of instruction from dancing master to pupil inherited by today's ballet instructors and students, then one can begin in the early fifteenth century with the appearance of a new aid for an old art—a dance instruction book. For the first time (in the 1440s, as far as is now known), a professional dancing master wrote down what to dance and how to dance it, thus allowing later generations to recreate, with substantial understanding, technique and choreography now over five hundred and fifty years old. Like manuals by subsequent authors, this treatise, *De arte saltandi e choreas ducendii* ("Of the art of leading *saltandi* and *choreas*")[1] by Domenico da Piacenza, did not forecast the future but described the inherited dance tradition of its own time. Thus it is possible that Domenico's dances represent an even earlier tradition, and it is certain that they did not expect to be connected to a then-unknown genre, classical ballet. Nonetheless, historian Ingrid Brainard points out that Domenico's choreographies include two miniature dance dramas, perhaps "the first two real ballets."[2]

BACKGROUND TO THE TRADITION

Without instruction books, a discussion of dance prior to the fifteenth century can be only speculation, advised by careful study of dance artifacts. These artifacts include evidence from musical scores, literary references, artistic depictions, clerical diatribes against dancing, philosophical advocacy for dancing, and a host of other secondary sources.

We know, for instance, from cave drawings that ancient peoples, sometimes costumed as animals, employed dance in a variety of ways. Judging by tribal dances today, movements were well organized and could be rhythmically complex, humorous as well as serious.

Egyptian tomb paintings depict solemn religious dancing of funeral processions patterned on the legend of the devoted Isis mourning for her beloved husband-brother, the god Osiris. Also portrayed are exuberant, acrobatic secular entertainments associated with those rites.

This dual nature of dance—ennobling and intoxicating—was evident in Greek culture also, as Plato noted:

> Movement of the body may be called dancing, and includes two kinds; one of the nobler figures, imitating the honorable, the other of the more ignoble figures, imitating the mean.[3]

Whether associated with gestures of the noble chorus in the great dramatic tragedies or the rowdy, satirical dances of comedies and satyr plays, Greek dancing cannot be reconstructed with any certainty—this in spite of the many visual sources, such as sculpture and vase decoration, documenting the integral place of dance in Greek life as private entertainment, communal activity, or religious ritual. Western theatrical dance has reflected, from the sixteenth century onward, Greek influence in thematic material and in costuming. Western education in the nineteenth and twentieth centuries has championed the benefits of dance to health and harmonious physical development, as did the ancient Greeks. The choice of *orchesis* (Greek for "dance") as the name of college dance clubs underscores that connection.[4]

Greek theatres (*theatron*, "place for seeing") have had their influence as well. They were outdoor amphitheatres, rising along a concave slope of a hill in a three-quarter circle of seats above a level, circular performance area called an *orchestra*. Behind that circular area, and opposite the spectators, was the *skene*, a structure whose facade provided a background, perhaps a temple, for the play, and whose interior served as a dressing area for the performers. Principal characters appeared from a central doorway, and entrances on either side provided other access.

As the Romans began conquering the surrounding countryside, they copied or adapted aspects of Greek drama and theatre, resulting in a gradual decline in the close relationship that dance had enjoyed with song, verse, and dramatic expression in the earlier hellenistic period. For an empire of peoples sharing no common language, for audiences who preferred exciting and colorful spectacles to classic dramatic forms, Roman theatrical fare developed danced interpretations emphasizing movement and gesture rather than verse and song. Highly skilled pantomime artists (*panto*, "all"; *mime*, "acting out") such as Pylades, a specialist in the tragic style, and Bathyllus, a comic virtuoso, enjoyed great wealth and considerable political power. The acrobatic nature of some of the *pantomimi* can be appreciated from written accounts at the time:

> He [the dancer] leaps on one foot then on both, stands on his right foot, and lifts his left leg up to his breast and shoulder, bends it round his back to his neck, whirls around, bent over backwards, so fast that his head seems to circle on the ground.[5]

Roman outdoor theatres were huge and opulent. The stage, raised about five feet high, could be as much as three hundred feet long and forty feet deep. The simple *skene* of Greek theatres became highly decorated facades whose columns and statuary could dwarf the performers. The orchestra area was reduced to a semicircle, used less for dancing than for seating important spectators or, on occasion, even flooded for performance of water spectacles.

A preference for spectacle over content saw the great pantomime artists gradually replaced by *mimi* specializing in lewd farces. These increasingly lascivious popular entertainments, along with circus games and gladiatorial combats, were denounced by the Church in Rome. Eventually, as Christian emperors replaced pagan ones and as the Church grew in power, dance in its various forms was, essentially, forbidden and the entertainers dispersed.

DANCE IN THE MIDDLE AGES

Even as the Church fathers preached against dancing as a form of bodily pleasure that impeded preparation for the spiritual afterlife, Christian theologians frequently employed dance imagery to extol the harmony of the universe and of the soul with that universe:

> The whole cosmos takes part in the dance. Whosoever does not take part in the dance does not know what shall come.[6]

The period from the fifth to the fourteenth century (from the decline of the Roman Empire to the beginning of the Renaissance), known as the Middle Ages, was not devoid of earthly dance. A variety of entertainers—jugglers, acrobats, conjurers, minstrels, and dancers—were familiar to medieval fairs, marketplaces, and village greens. Of these, the minstrel, who sang and played an instrument, was a kind of voice for society in the absence of theatres and before the invention of the printing press. He could pass along the great legends, epic poems, and ballads of mankind as well as satirize the established order—clergy, aristocrats, and peasants.

The Church, whose authority was thus challenged, could not succeed in censoring such popular entertainments, and gradually it sanctioned certain dramatic elements into its own liturgy. As a method of dramatizing biblical stories, the lives of saints, and moral lessons, these mystery, miracle, and morality plays at first were produced within the church basilica itself. The manuscript for one such liturgical music-drama, the *Planctus Mariae* ("The Lament of Mary"), produced in the fourteenth century in northern Italy, contains seventy-nine directions for movement and gesture, written above the text and interspersed with the musical staves.[7] While not exactly a description of dance, the multitude of movement directions for the four characters does allow a certain authentic restaging of this late medieval work.

Although subject matter remained religious, the presentation manner became increasingly secular, designed for entertainment as the plays moved out of the church proper into the streets and marketplaces. Performers were members of a guild and traveled from town to town setting up their booths or "mansions" for performances.

In France, in 1330, journeymen jugglers and minstrels decided to form their own guild, following the example of other trades and in recognition of their increasing popularity as entertainers for an aristocracy growing in wealth and worldliness.[8] Dramatic changes in medieval life had begun in the eleventh century as the hold of the Church loosened. The rise of the towns, establishment of universities, development of large-scale commerce, and exchange with other cultures during the Crusades all contributed to the flowering of European civilization. A new moral system, chivalry, developed at the same time as the Crusades (eleventh–thirteenth centuries). As a code uniting religious and military predilections, it profoundly affected aristocratic life. Idealizing romantic love, ennobling men and improving the status of women, encouraging cleanliness, witty conversation, elegance, and courteous manners, it influenced castle social life, including the taste for art songs and refined social dances. Thus, "minstrels and jugglers had progressively relinquished their monkeys and their bears, concentrating on refining their skills as dancers and choreographers to suit the demands of a more polished and sophisticated society."[9]

By the early fifteenth century, a distinction was made between those musicians who played a treble fiddle and instructed dancing, and those who played a bass fiddle in a band. Both the minstrel-dancers and the band members remained within the same guild, headed by the "king of the violins."[10] Indeed, the violin, played by the dancing master himself, continued to be the instrument for accompanying dance classes and ballet lessons until the twentieth century.

SOCIAL AND THEATRICAL DANCES OF THE RENAISSANCE

This brings us once again to Domenico da Piacenza, author of *De arte saltandi e choreas ducendii,* the earliest extant dance instruction book. Like his French counterparts, Domenico was skilled both in music and dance. The content of his manual, like that of many in the next centuries, gives us an idea of the skills and duties expected of dancing masters at court. For instance, they were theoreticians: "Dancing is the synthesis of movement and space and music . . . if you do justice to these elements, the result will be true dancing. . . ." But if not, Domenico goes on to say, you will not be more than a "mere stamper of the feet."[11]

In addition to giving daily dance instruction to their noble patrons, dancing masters, regarded as experts on proper social behavior, also taught correct ballroom manners, including how to dress properly, how to bow correctly, and how to handle one's gloves, hat, fan, or sword with ease. All were requisites for advancement in courtly circles. We might call this elegant, effortless-looking deportment the "courtesy of grand manners," an attribute still reflected today in the posture and bearing of the classically trained ballet dancer.

The dancing master was expected to devise new dances for the ballroom and for court festivals, where he might also perform along with his noble pupils. Choreographies were documented in a variety of ways: explanations in prose, shorthand symbols, and initial letters or abbreviations of step names. Fifteenth-century French sources depict the elegant, gliding *basse danse,* performed by one couple, or by several partners in procession. Despite a limited vocabulary of five movements (*révérence,* single, double, *reprise,* and *branle*), *basses danses* had subtle and sophisticated performance qualities. The Italian counterpart, the *bassadanza,* offered more variety in choreographic pattern, step sequence, and number of participants. Even greater variation was achieved in the *ballo,* a dance piece for a specified number of dancers, featuring frequent changes of musical rhythm and sometimes possibilities for dramatic expression.

Italian festival art developed the *intermezzi,* spectacular musico-dramatic interludes inserted between the acts of lengthy plays, at first revivals of ancient comedies. Originating in the late fifteenth century in Ferrara, the *intermezzi* came to include elaborate mechanical marvels of scenic effects; brilliantly costumed actors, singers, and dancers; and the coordinated efforts of poets, composers, designers, and choreographers. During the sixteenth century, thematic material for the *intermezzi* (usually four to six in number) became more unified and sometimes related directly to the play. Their chief purposes, however, were to edify and entertain the spectators and to enhance the prestige of the host. The

Handsome dance manuals such as *Le gratie d'amore* ("The graces of love," 1602) by Cesare Negri document the highly developed dance technique of Italian courtiers. Typically the dances began with a *riverenza* or bow as in this *balletto.*

COURTESY OF THE BROUDE BROTHERS, LTD., FACSIMILE EDITION.

most elaborate examples were the *intermezzi* of 1589, devised to accompany the comedy *La Pellegrina,* one of the entertainments surrounding the wedding festivities in Florence for Ferdinando de' Medici and Christine of Lorraine. Overseeing the entire production was Emilio de' Cavalieri, a composer, organist, voice teacher, dancer, choreographer, administrator, and diplomat! His choreographic instructions for the final *ballo* (for four women, three men, and a singing chorus that also moved) have survived, providing a rare example of sixteenth-century theatrical dance.

The step vocabulary used by Cavalieri can be understood from descriptions of similar movements by other Italian dancing masters of the period, notably Fabritio Caroso (*Il ballarino,* Venice, 1581, and *Nobiltà di dame,* Venice, 1600) and Cesare Negri (*Le gratie d'amore,* Milan, 1602). Their treatises include choreographies for dozens of social dances (Negri also has a few theatrical ones), written in prose form, with their music, written in lute tablature. Typically beginning and ending with a gracious *riverenza* or bow, the repertory includes examples of the *balletto,* a couple dance with several sections in contrasting rhythm. An introductory passage, perhaps a stately *pavana* in duple meter (two or four beats to a bar of music), is followed by a triple-meter *gagliarda*, in which first the gentleman does a solo of leaps, beats, and jumps, and then the lady performs a variation in a more restrained yet lively manner. A brisker *saltarello* for both dancers leads to the finale, the exuberant *canario* with toe-heel brushes and stamps in intricate rhythms.[12]

The structure for such sixteenth-century *balletti* for a *cavaliere* and his lady is not unlike that of the ballet *pas de deux* for a *danseur* and ballerina. Beginning as it does with an *entrée* and *adagio* for the couple, the *pas de deux* proceeds to exciting variations performed first by the male dancer and then by his partner, and is brought to conclusion in the lively coda for both. The technique is markedly different, however. Renaissance dancers did not point the feet or turn out the legs. Dancing side by side or face to face, partners seldom touched except for an occasional holding or slapping of hands. Indeed, only movements for the legs are described in this period. Their intricacy, however, required practice, and Negri's illustrations show a courtier holding onto a table and a chair, the better to execute his leg movements.

Judging by engravings of the *intermezzi*, theatrical dances for joyous, peaceful scenes were symmetrical and orderly, no doubt performed with the effortless grace espoused for proper social dancing. By contrast, inferno scenes show disorganized, irregular groupings. We can only conjecture what the movement might have been for grotesque or for humorous interludes. Court choreographers may have gleaned ideas from groups of itinerant entertainers, practitioners of *commedia dell'arte* ("comedy of skill") that originated about the mid-sixteenth century. Often parodying court behavior, these professional actors were skilled musicians and dancers as well. Their dynamic quality and popular stock characters, such as Harlequin and Columbine, appear as frequent influences in ballet's technical and artistic history, but documentation of their early dances does not remain.

Lost, too, are the genuine early folk dances of peasants, artisans, and villagers, for the material in the dance manuals reflects only the practice of the courts and upper classes. Yet, through the years, folk and national dances have been lively sources for ballet choreographers to call on. Some vestige of their quality in the Renaissance comes from *Orchesography*, published in 1589 by Thoinot Arbeau, a pseudonym for Jehan Tabourot, a canon in the Roman Catholic Church at Langres. Neither a dancing master nor employee of a royal patron, this scholarly churchman nevertheless wrote an important instruction book of dances standard with the gentry and nobility of the French provinces. Far less complex than the Italian repertory, some of the dances, the many *branles*, for example, may have an even more humble background. Performed with simple steps and hops in a circle or chain formation by several couples, the *branles* may be descendants of the medieval *carole* or *chorea*. Another dance described by Arbeau, the *volta* ("turning"), is a variation of the *galliard* but is distinguished by its hearty turns in which the gentleman lifts his partner.

Arbeau's book, written in the form of a conversation with a student, Capriol, emphasizes courteous social behavior and correct execution of dance technique, including proper positions of the feet and legs. Bearing faint resemblance to ballet's positions of the feet, Arbeau's positions are illustrated showing only slight turnout. He believed that although "the degree [of turnout] is left to the discretion of the dancer . . . the natural rotation of the leg will not permit it to exceed a right angle."[13] Similar positions were used for fencing, which, along with dancing and riding, were requisite accomplishments for any gentleman.

More sophisticated dances were typical of the French royal courts. Beginning with the marriage in 1533 of Catherine de Médici, daughter of one of the greatest families of Italy, and Henri, duc d'Orléans, three years later the king of France, Italian dancing masters were employed by the French monarchy. As queen, and later as queen mother following the untimely death of Henri, Catherine promoted lavish entertainments as much to celebrate events of the royal household as to reinforce her political policies. Costly festivals of several days' duration might include banquets, water shows, firework displays, and balls. Composite entertainments of verse, music, dance, and decor were devised to highlight the occasion. These developed into the genre known as *ballet de cour* ("court ballet") and, to maximize their effect, they became increasingly the responsibility of learned advisors, such as Jean-Antoine de Baif, who advocated the unity of music, verse, and dance—following the example of ancient Greece. To further these goals, a French royal patent in 1570 recognized the efforts of de Baif by establishing the Académie de Poésie et de Musique.

Three years later a festival honoring the naming of Catherine's son as king of Poland featured an hour-long ballet devised for sixteen ladies of the court, representing the sixteen provinces of France. Their flawless execution of numerous geometrical patterns so impressed the visiting Polish ambassadors that they declared that no other court on earth could possibly imitate the French dance. The production reflected the work of Baldassare di Belgioioso, who had arrived from Italy in 1555 as a member of a band of violins, and then, changing his name to Beaujoyeulx, became producer of entertainments at Catherine's court.

Perhaps the greatest achievement of Beaujoyeulx and the academicians was the 1581 production of the *Balet Comique de la Royne*, one of many magnificences honoring the marriage of the sister of Catherine's daughter-in-law. According to Beaujoyeulx, the title of the ballet (literally, "The Queen's Comedy-Ballet") was chosen more for the "beautiful, tranquil and happy conclusion than for the quality of the personages, who are almost all gods and goddesses, or other heroic persons."[14]

The plot, a story of the enchantress Circe, whose evil spells finally were broken by intervention of the gods (identified with the royal family), was unfolded by a succession of verses, songs, and dances that gave a certain dramatic unity to the production. The libretto, the music, and several engravings of the elaborate costumes and pageant cars (rather like parade floats, pulled by several men) were published, but, alas, not the choreography. Beaujoyeulx proudly wrote some description of the final dance, however, a *grand ballet* of

> forty passages or geometric figures . . . sometimes square, sometimes round, . . . then in triangles accompanied by a small square. . . . At the middle of the Ballet a chain was formed, composed of four interlacings, each different from the others. . . . The spectators thought that Archimedes could not have understood geometric proportions any better than the princesses and the ladies observed in this Ballet.[15]

Under the influence of the Académie, not only the dance patterns of the ballets but also their steps, music, and verses were closely correlated to produce the greatest symbolic impact, capable of imparting philosophical principles. "Dancing was no frivolous pastime, but an intensive intellectual experience for both dancer and spectator."[16]

By the 1580s in Italy, permanent theatres were being built, adaptations of earlier Roman designs, with perspective painting added to the stage. Inclined ramps connected the stage to the floor of the auditorium, and all three areas could be utilized for performance. In France, however, entertainments such as the *Ballet Comique* occurred in the center floor of large rooms of a palace. Royal dignitaries sat at one end of the hall, and performers and decorative pageant cars entered at the opposite end. Along the sides were raised galleries accommodating sometimes thousands of spectators watching the dance patterns unfold.

The English equivalent to the Italian *intermezzi* and the French *ballet de cour* was the court masque, usually based on a mythological or allegorical theme adapted to extol the virtues of the monarchy. Enhanced by scenic wonders devised by stage architect Inigo Jones and verses by poet laureate Ben Jonson, masques offered a succession of songs, speeches, and dances performed by elaborately costumed members of the court. Noble, serious characters of the masque proper were contrasted with demons, furies, and nymphs in antimasque sections of the production. Members of the audience were invited to join the masquers in general dancing, called revels. Social dancing by the entire assembly frequently terminated theatrical evenings in Italy and France as well. A favorite English form was the country dance, a lively circle or longways dance for several couples at once. Choreographies and music for these pleasurable dances were collected and published in 1651 in John Playford's *The English Dancing Master*. The English love of dancing is apparent in the many references to dance by Shakespeare in his plays, such as in *Henry V* when Bourbon declares, "They bid us to the English dancing schools and teach lavoltas, high and swift corantos." However, following the Puritan overthrow of the English monarchy in 1640, theatrical activities and court masques were suspended. Italian taste turned to the development of opera, an outgrowth of the *intermezzi*. But in France, the ballet was to enter an important new phase.

Members of the aristocracy took part in elaborate court entertainments featuring dancing in intricate geometric patterns as in this scene from the first *intermezzo* of *La Liberazione di Tireno e d'Arnea* ("The liberation of Tyrsenus and Arnea," 1617) held in the Medici theatre of the Uffizi Palace in Florence. Note the variety of performance levels—auditorium floor, ramps, stage, and suspended scenery.

COURTESY OF THE DANCE COLLECTION, THE NEW YORK PUBLIC LIBRARY AT LINCOLN CENTER, ASTOR, LENOX AND TILDEN FOUNDATIONS.

BIRTH OF THE CLASSICAL BALLET

The long reign of Louis XIV (1643–1715) brought *ballet de cour* to its most brilliant phase but also contributed to its demise in favor of the establishment of a fully professional theatrical enterprise. The king, himself a nimble dancer appearing in court ballets over a period of eighteen years and continuing daily dance lessons for many more, excelled as patron of the arts. In bringing together and encouraging first-rate composers, choreographers, dancers, designers, and poets, the royal dancer-patron-impressario intended that court functions would provide a diverting occupation for his courtiers and an impressive display of cultured magnificence for all Europe.

An early and crucial appointment was that of Jean-Baptiste Lully as composer responsible for the music for court ballets. Having learned to play the guitar in his native Italy, Lully arrived in France as a young teenager and soon showed prowess as violinist and dancer, attracting notice by the court. He danced alongside the young Louis XIV in an elaborate, all-night fête, the *Ballet de la Nuit,* in which the fourteen-year-old king first appeared in the role of Apollo, the sun god. A sumptuous example of *ballet à entrée,* the production had four acts, each with a separate plot, composer, and numerous *entrées* ("entrances") interspersed with spoken lines. Typically, most dancers were members of the court. Gradually, as Lully was granted more control, court productions became more integrated unities, and professional dancers, including women, assumed more roles. One virtuoso dancer (and accomplished violinist as well), Pierre Beauchamps, was to have an important place in ballet's formative years. His dance specialty was the *tourbillon,* described by a contemporary as a movement in which he "throws his feet forward and makes a turn in the air."[17]

Beauchamps made his debut as a choreographer in 1661 in the *comédie-ballet, Les Facheux* ("The Bores"), a new theatre form created by Jean-Baptiste Poquelin, better known by his stage name, Molière. Intending to have dances during the intervals of the acts of his verse play, but given only two weeks to mount the production, Molière instead decided that "in order not to break the thread of the comedy by these sorts of *intermèdes,* it was thought judicious to tack them on to the subject and to make one thing of the ballet and the play. . . .[18] Thus did expediency lead Molière and Beauchamps to use dance as a means of enhancing the actual development of the plot, not merely as a diversion, and to encourage dancers to be more expressive in their dancing, as well as to gesture and pose appropriately during the action of the play. It was a course they followed in other productions, *Le Bourgeois Gentilhomme* ("The Gentleman Citizen," 1670) being probably best known today, but seldom performed with its music or dance possibilities.

In 1661, the year of Louis XIV's ascension to absolute power, the king showed his concern with raising the quality of dancing by establishing the Académie Royale de Danse. Thirteen of the most experienced dancing masters were appointed to set artistic standards for teaching and training dancers for court ballets. Granted independent power to license teachers, the academicians were violently opposed by the musicians' guild, to which dancers had belonged for three centuries. A deeper issue was the divorce of the arts from one another, breaking the unity espoused by Renaissance philosophers.

Creation of dance specialists was deemed timely, however, as ballets took on greater theatrical aspects. One of these was the moving of ballet productions from the ballroom floor onto a raised stage. Giacomo Torelli, an Italian scene designer invited to work at the court in Paris, advocated establishment of the proscenium arch as a stage frame enhancing his use of machines to shift scenes quickly. Such a theatre, the Palais Royale, was given over for performances by the Académie Royale de Musique, a performing institution (later known as the Paris Opéra) established by Louis XIV in 1672 to be headed by his protégé, Lully. Pierre Beauchamps, by now director of the dancers' academy, was appointed dancing master to the music academy, thus in effect merging the two institutions.

Performers, no longer surrounded by their audience, needed to rely less on symbolic formations of large groups and more on the agility and design of an individual body watched by spectators out front. Precise movements and poses required more codification of the step vocabulary. The establishment of the five

During the seventeenth century, theatrical productions receded behind the confines of the proscenium stage, as in this performance at Versailles. Performers were well aware of the royal personages seated directly opposite stage center. This "comedy in music," *Les Fêtes de l'Amour et de Bacchus* ("The Festival of Love and Bacchus," first presented in 1672 and revived at intervals until 1738), was based on a text by Molière, with music by Lully and dances by Beauchamps.

COURTESY OF THE DANCE COLLECTION, THE NEW YORK PUBLIC LIBRARY AT LINCOLN CENTER, ASTOR, LENOX AND TILDEN FOUNDATIONS.

positions for the feet, still foundational for today's ballet technique, is credited to Beauchamps, who "found that nothing was more important to maintain the body in a graceful attitude and the steps in a fixed space than to introduce these five positions."[19] Basic to their design was turnout of the leg, already a requirement for "a handsome carriage of the leg . . . regarded as a necessity of elegant bearing" among seventeenth-century nobility and gentry, as well as dancers.[20] The angle of turnout, when heels touched and toes turned outward, was about 90 degrees. Complete 180-degree turnout was still a century away.

Preservation of choreography continued to be a problem, and Louis XIV requested Pierre Beauchamps, who had become the monarch's dance instructor, to try to devise a method of notating dance movement. By 1700, the long-awaited notation system was completed and published, not by Beauchamps,

The far-ranging influence of French dance technique was enhanced by the development and publication of a notation system for recording movement. This frontispiece from a German dance manual, *Rechtschaffener Tantzmeister* ("The Worthy Dancing Master," 1717), by Gottfried Taubert, depicts a dancing master with his notation at his library desk while his dancers, perhaps in his imagination, rehearse in the foreground.

COURTESY OF THE DANCE COLLECTION, THE NEW YORK PUBLIC LIBRARY AT LINCOLN CENTER, ASTOR, LENOX AND TILDEN FOUNDATIONS.

however, but by another choreographer, Raoul Anger Feuillet. In his treatise, *Chorégraphie,* symbols rather than words indicated positions, steps, and the various movements of the dance: *plié, elevé, sauté, cabriole, tombé, glissé, tourné,* as well as cadence or time, and the figure or pattern of the dance. The French terminology of the Académie Royale de Danse became standard for the rest of the Western dance world, but the execution of the various steps has, in most cases, changed considerably. Nevertheless, by means of the notation system and helpful manuals[21] from the early eighteenth century, the charming dances of that period can be reconstructed with considerable accuracy. Published along with *Chorégraphie* were notations of theatrical dances composed by Feuillet (including a ballet for nine dancers) and ballroom dances by Guillaume Louis Pécour, Beauchamps's successor at the Académie. For the next twenty-five years, annual collections of dances were published and eagerly sought to learn the latest ballroom dances, thus preparing for the coming social season, and to keep up with what was happening in theatrical dance.

Dance technique of both amateur and professional remained essentially the same, differing only in the degree of difficulty expected for stage performance. Judging by the elaborate choreography for esteemed performers such as Balon, Blondy, and Marcel, or Mlles Subligny, Guiot, and Prévost, the technical level for ballet was indeed high. Difficult maneuvers of acrobatic nature were depicted in Gregorio Lambranzi's *New and Curious School of Theatrical Dancing* (Nurenberg, 1716).

By the time notated dances appeared, the noble and intellectually demanding *courante*, favorite of Louis XIV, had been replaced in popularity by the livelier, but still subtle and elegant, *minuet.*[22] Theatrical dances included these and other social dance forms, such as *gigues, canaries, sarabandes, gavottes,* and *bourrées. Contredanses,* the French embellishment on English country dancing, gained in popularity in the ballroom. Over three hundred and fifty notated dances exist from the Baroque period and can be reconstructed today.

Movements for the hands and opposition of arms to legs became standardized. Indeed, such were the regulations and influence established by the Paris Opéra throughout Europe that it is not surprising to hear rumblings of discontent.

EIGHTEENTH-CENTURY PROFESSIONALISM AND REFORM

Stage dancers were now professionals, but their strictly codified movement and costuming, only slightly modified to suit any one production, continued to reflect their courtly heritage. One highly popular performance vehicle of the early part of the century was the opera-ballet, a musical production of singing, dancing, and scenic display. In works such as *Les Festes Vénitiennes* (1710) with music by André Campra and choreography by Pécour, opera-ballet offered artistic as well as popular appeal. But some restless dancers and ballet masters envisioned dramatic dance performances without dependence on either words or song to relate a scenario. Such innovative experiments took place outside the Paris Opéra domain.

In 1717, John Weaver, an English dance master and theoretician, attempted a wholly danced drama, the *Loves of Mars and Venus,* as a revival of practices "from the Ancients, in Imitation of their Pantomime."[23] Also in London, a young French dancer of exceptional expressive ability, Marie Sallé, broke several traditions: She challenged the male dominance in choreography by composing the ballet *Pygmalion* (1734), in which she dared challenge standard costuming as well, appearing "without pannier [hoops around the hips], skirt, or bodice, and with her hair down. . . . Apart from her corset and petticoat she wore only a simple dress of muslin draped about her in the manner of a Greek statue."[24] Sallé's reforms were in an effort to achieve greater realism and expression in ballet. Her rival for favor among the highly vociferous ballet fans was Marie-Anne de Cupis de Camargo, a reformer in her own way but for different reasons. A highly skilled technician, Camargo resented the freedom that costuming afforded male dancers, thus allowing their unencumbered legs to show off virtuoso steps. So Camargo shortened her hooped-skirted dress several scandalous inches—to the calf of her leg. *Caleçons de précaution* (tight-fitting drawers) preserved modesty during her jumps and beats.

Prior to the French Revolution, a typical eighteenth-century ballet costume for a male dancer included a plumed headdress and a *tonnelet* or wired skirt not unlike the ballet tutu later worn by female dancers. For women, a tightly laced corset, a long skirt held out by wire frames at the hip or along the petticoat, and heeled shoes were deemed suitable for any role.

COURTESY OF THE DANCE COLLECTION, THE NEW YORK PUBLIC LIBRARY AT LINCOLN CENTER, ASTOR, LENOX AND TILDEN FOUNDATIONS.

Of the many ballet masters who challenged the status quo, only Jean Georges Noverre made the effort to publish his complaints and suggestions. His *Lettres sur la danse et sur les ballets* (1760) urged dancers to "renounce *cabrioles*, *entrechats*, and overcomplicated steps . . . away with those lifeless masks . . . take off those enormous wigs . . . discard the use of those stiff cumbersome hoops. . . . Renounce that slavish routine which keeps your art in its infancy . . . gracefully set aside the narrow laws of a school to follow the impressions of nature. . . ."[25]

Even as he quarreled with much of his dance heritage, Noverre, a student of the elegant "god of the dance," Louis Dupré, did not wish to reject all that had gone on before. For instance, "In order to dance well," he said, "nothing is so important as the turning outward of the thigh."[26] But for Noverre, movements of the legs, no matter how brilliant, were only a part of true dancing, where "everything must speak; each gesture, each attitude, each *port de bras* must possess a different expression."[27]

Noverre elaborated his ideas as ballet master in Stuttgart. Later, in Vienna, he collaborated with composer Christoph Gluck, who was experimenting in similar ways in opera. One of Noverre's finest ballets, *Jason et Medée,* was staged at the Paris Opéra in 1770 and later in London by another pupil of Dupré, Gaetano Vestris, a renowned dancer who had worked with Noverre. In 1776, the queen of France, Marie Antoinette, a former pupil of Noverre in her native Vienna, succeeded in having Noverre appointed ballet master at the Paris Opéra, a position he had long coveted.

Noverre created some one hundred and fifty ballets during his long career,

The climactic scene of Noverre's dramatic *ballet d'action, Jason et Medée,* is shown in its 1781 London staging by Gaetano Vestris, celebrated dancer of the noble style, who danced the role of Jason, the faithless lover.

COURTESY OF THE DANCE COLLECTION, THE NEW YORK PUBLIC LIBRARY AT LINCOLN CENTER, ASTOR, LENOX AND TILDEN FOUNDATIONS.

but none survive. He disdained notation, but in any case the old Feuillet system, adequate as it was for earlier divertissements, was not able to accommodate the innovations of *ballet d'action*, in which a dramatic plot was conveyed entirely in movement and gesture.

However, a gently comic ballet by one of Noverre's outstanding pupils, Jean Dauberval, has survived. *La Fille Mal Gardée* ("The Ill-Guarded Girl") was produced in Bordeaux just two weeks before the outbreak of the French Revolution in July 1789. This timely ballet featured peasants as heroes and depicted real-life situations using a dance style that blended the academic technique of the time with folk dance elements. The ballet soon enjoyed success on stages from London to St. Petersburg, and it still is performed today, notably by Britain's Royal Ballet, in versions true, if not to Dauberval's original steps, at least to his carefully constructed plot and delightful characters.

At the close of the eighteenth century, *ballet d'action* had proved it could relate a story without relying on words or song. Dancing was capable of more than mere divertissement within an opera or drama. Ballets could hold the stage alone, even if they were typically given following, or between the acts of, some other theatrical event.

The wearing of masks to help portray characters, a tradition of ancient origin, was abolished by 1772, allowing facial expression to become more important. Fashion implemented by the French Revolution replaced cumbersome courtly dress and rigid corsets with lighter, more flowing costumes based on Greek and Roman drapery. Greater freedom of movement, especially for the upper body and arms, allowed gesture to become "more natural," a goal of the dance reformers.

At La Scala in Milan, Salvatore Viganò extended the ideas of Noverre and Dauberval to include more individualized expression, even for the *corps de ballet*, which heretofore had moved mostly in symmetrical unison. Viganò's grandiose conceptions, in which he strove to "involve the heart" as well as please the eyes, attracted strong support from some (Beethoven composed his only ballet score, *The Creatures of Prometheus*, for him), but others, such as composer Rossini, complained that his ballets contained "too much pantomime and not enough dancing."[28]

Dance technique as well as style had been affected by changes in costume. For women especially, shucking of the long hooped skirts allowed a freedom of leg movement hitherto not imagined, plus the possibility for supported *adagio*, for now their partners could get close enough to hold them. Charles Didelot, a faithful student of Dauberval, extended the concept of partnering, including simple lifts and movements that emphasized strength for the male and lightness for the female. By an ingenious system of almost-invisible wires, his lightly clad dancers could be raised, lowered, or flown across the stage, an apt device for his highly popular ballet *Flore et Zéphyre* (1796), the love story of a nymph and the breeze of the West Wind.

Also appearing in London in that 1781 season was Gaetano's son, Auguste Vestris, whose technical virtuosity could not be denied even by this English caricature. Through his dazzling performances as a youth and his long career as a teacher, Auguste Vestris exerted a great influence on the development of ballet technique on the eve of the romantic period.

COURTESY OF THE DANCE COLLECTION, THE NEW YORK PUBLIC LIBRARY AT LINCOLN CENTER, ASTOR, LENOX AND TILDEN FOUNDATIONS.

But having discarded heeled shoes in favor of heelless sandals or slippers, dancers were achieving a new elevation on their own. Outstanding for his sensational jumps, beats, and turns was Auguste Vestris, son of the celebrated Gaetano. Unlike his father, who inherited the elegant, noble style of his teacher, Dupré, Auguste excelled in dazzling virtuoso displays of skill. Steps of almost acrobatic nature, once the specialty of comic or grotesque dancers, are documented in Gennaro Magri's *Trattato teorico-prattico di ballo* ("theoretical and practical treatise of the ballet," Naples, 1779).

The Paris Opéra had long endeavored to enforce strict observance of three distinct dance styles, including designation of proper physique for each. For the noble style, a dancer's structure should be stately and well-proportioned because he would be destined for serious, heroic roles, for gods such as Apollo (or Venus, if a woman). The *demi-caractère* dancer could be of medium height, still elegant but adept at a variety of virtuoso styles appropriate for lesser gods such as Mercury or Zéphir. The comic or grotesque dancer could be of indifferent stature, even thickset, but necessarily strong. His roles were of a rustic or pastoral nature and could include steps and dances characteristic of various national or folklore sources, the so-called character dances such as the bolero and tarantella.

But, as in the case of Auguste Vestris, who became an influential teacher in the early nineteenth century, such distinctions of the old order were beginning to break down, just as steps and styles were evolving toward a different form. What was yet lacking was the artistic impetus to make use of these newly developing skills.

THE GOLDEN AGE OF ROMANTIC BALLET

An artistic push did come along; the romantic movement was felt in ballet no less than in literature, music, and painting. For ballet, it was a liberation from strict thematic and technical conventions of previous eras, stubbornly continued at the Paris Opéra. Basic subjects of romanticism came from the perceived conflicts between beauty and ugliness, good and evil, spirit and flesh. With themes juxtaposing realism and fantasy, mortal with supernatural, romantic ballet wanted—and had it—both ways: to be a vehicle for real drama and a showcase for masters of technique.

The aerial flights provided by Didelot's wires were ideal for the spiritual creatures of the new ballets, but dancers wished to create ethereal illusion by their own movements. Since it was the woman who was cast in the role of unattainable supernatural creature, it was she who desired to dance on the least possible earthly surface, the very tips of her toes. But wishing alone would not make it so. "Romantic themes could be danced onstage only after the mastery of a rational and ordered technical system."[29]

Such a system had been evolving during the last decades of the previous century, but not until 1820 was there "any really valuable literature upon the subject of dancing." So said the young dancer Carlo Blasis in his *Elementary Treatise upon the Theory and Practice of the Art of Dancing,*[30] the first published account of ballet technique as we recognize it today, including the first outline of the structure of a ballet class. Blasis, who had worked with Dauberval and Viganò, urged dancers to "be as light as possible. . . . I would like to see you bound with a suppleness and agility which gives me the impression you are barely touching the ground and may at any moment take flight."[31] And his rigorous method of training made the impossible happen. As described in more detail by his disciple, Giovanni Léopold Adice,[32] Blasis's *barre* work included, in the order given, 48 *pliés*, 128 *grand battements*, 96 *petits battements* (like *battements tendus* today), 128 *ronds de jambe à terre* and the same *en l'air*, 64 slow *petits battements sur le cou-de-pied*, and 120 rapid ones. These were "preliminary" exercises, to be repeated in center floor before going on to the rest of the lesson!

Illustrations in Blasis's *Treatise* and his later *Code of Terpsichore* (London, 1828) show dancers in complete 180-degree turnout but, surprisingly, no dancer

Newly installed gas lighting enhanced the Paris Opéra premiere of Meyerbeer's opera *Robert le Diable* ("Robert the Devil," 1831), especially this ballet scene, in which the ghosts of nuns rise from their graves to lure Robert. Featuring Marie Taglioni in choreography by her father, the opera's ballet scenes were early examples of the romantic era's fascination with the supernatural and exotic.

COURTESY OF THE DANCE COLLECTION, THE NEW YORK PUBLIC LIBRARY AT LINCOLN CENTER, ASTOR, LENOX AND TILDEN FOUNDATIONS.

Amalia Brugnoli was one of the first to dance on the point of her foot, performing "very extraordinary things," according to Marie Taglioni, who saw her in 1822. Brugnoli, shown here with her husband, dancer-choreographer Paolo Samengo, also studied and danced with Carlo Blasis, whose school at La Scala produced many of the extraordinary technicians of nineteenth-century ballet.

COURTESY OF THE DANCE COLLECTION, THE NEW YORK PUBLIC LIBRARY AT LINCOLN CENTER, ASTOR, LENOX AND TILDEN FOUNDATIONS.

on full point. Yet prints from the turn of the nineteenth century depict such dancers as Fanny Bias, Amalia Brugnoli, and Maria De (or Del) Caro poised on the extreme points of their toes. But point work as such was not generally in use, nor was its revolutionary nature fully realized. E. A. Théleur, an English dancer and teacher who trained in France and Frenchified his name from Taylor, indicated several movements that could be done either "on the balls of the feet or the tips of the toes." His book *Letters on Dancing* (London, 1831) is the first dance text to actually show illustrations of women on toetip, and it is the first nineteenth-century attempt to devise a new system of dance notation. Like Blasis before, Théleur asserts that heels should never leave the floor in *pliés* and advocates the correct maximum height of the leg as hip level.

This was the training typical at the time Marie Taglioni prepared for her debut in 1822. Arduously trained by her father, Filippo, Marie Taglioni epitomized the newly developing style: Her delicate *relevé* to full point replaced the deliberate rise to half-toe of the previous century; one leg extended slightly backward became a waist-high *arabesque* and, with the other foot poised *en pointe*, a symbolic yearning to soar upward. To the previous emphasis on *terre à terre* steps ("ground to ground," meaning the feet scarcely leave the floor) was added the *ballonnée* style with its high and effortless-appearing jumps and leaps.

To show off his daughter's superb skills, Filippo Taglioni created many ballets, including his masterpiece, *La Sylphide* (Paris, 1832), a story of a desirable but unreachable sylph pursued by an infatuated young Scotsman, who, hapless mortal that he was, inadvertently killed his beloved. In the soft glow of gaslights, Taglioni, clothed in a full skirt of the lightest gauze reaching to mid-calf, seemed to float about the huge opera house stage with her soaring, silent *jetés*, her incredibly smooth movements and delicate balances. The theme and setting of *La Sylphide* and the costume, technique, and personality of Marie Taglioni ushered in the golden age of romantic ballet and created a style still popular today. One of the most frequently performed ballets in America has been *Les Sylphides*, a neoromantic storyless ballet created by Michel Fokine to the music of Chopin seventy-six years after *La Sylphide.*

A ballerina is never without rivals, and there were many who wished to share the spotlight with Taglioni. One of the most successful challengers was Fanny Elssler, a Viennese beauty whose specialty was a kind of theatrical folk dancing, done with the sparkle and precision of a highly skilled ballet dancer. Perhaps her greatest success was in *La Cachucha,* a Spanish-style dance that much later was notated by Friederich A. Zorn in *Grammar of the Art of Dancing* (Odessa, 1887). (Spanish influences had been felt in social and theatrical dancing since the Renaissance; ballet dancers routinely played castanets.) When Taglioni accepted an invitation to dance in St. Petersburg, Elssler remained in Paris to enjoy the role of undisputed star of the Opéra. Two years later, in 1840, Elssler crossed the Atlantic for a three-month American tour that was extended to two years. Audiences in New York, Philadelphia, and Baltimore rivaled each other in

Fanny Elssler charmed audiences in the United States as well as in all of Europe with her passionate dancing, especially in *La Cachucha* (1836), a Spanish-style solo complete with castanet playing. This portrait accompanied the New York publication of the sheet music for that dance.

AUTHOR'S COLLECTION.

their adulation for Elssler and her fiery dances; Congress adjourned for her performances in Washington.

The spiritual Taglioni and the sensual Elssler split the artistic world into two passionate factions, reminiscent of the Sallé-Camargo rivalry a century before. But another ballerina came along who offered the public *both* qualities, moreover in the same ballet; she was Carlotta Grisi, and the ballet was *Giselle.* First performed in 1841, *Giselle* is a universally touching story, perfectly constructed, with a role that tempts, and thereby challenges, every ballerina. It tells of a simple peasant girl, Giselle, who is betrayed in love, goes mad with grief, and kills herself. But that is only Act I. By Act II, Giselle has become one of the Wilis, the spirits of betrothed girls who have died as maidens. At midnight the Wilis rise from their graves to attract young men into their midst, only to compel them to dance until they fall dead with exhaustion. But Giselle saves her deceitful (now repentant) lover from such a fate by offering to dance in his place. This scenario was developed from an old German legend by several men, including

Théophile Gautier, a poet turned ballet critic, whose great admiration for Carlotta Grisi glowed from his windy, flowery reviews. Jean Coralli did the choreography, with solo passages for Mlle Grisi composed by Jules Perrot, one of the few male dancers of the romantic era to receive much attention from the public or press, although his contributions to *Giselle* went unacknowledged at the time. Adolphe Adam composed a score that gave leading characters identifiable melodic themes throughout the ballet.

An American dancer, Mary Ann Lee, traveled to Europe to study and then hurried back home to dance *Giselle* in Boston in 1846. Her contemporary, Augusta Maywood, extended a European visit to a lifetime career, becoming the first American dancer to achieve fame and fortune abroad.

The ballerina had become the undisputed star of the ballet stage. Four of these talented, temperamental ladies were persuaded to dance together in 1845. Their short ballet, *Pas de Quatre*, was a masterpiece of choreographic diplomacy by Perrot, who managed to display the individual skills of the dancers without offending the pride of any one of them. It was agreed that Taglioni should be awarded the place of honor, the final variation of the ballet. The others, after tempestuous argument on the day of the performance, finally agreed to appear in order of their age: first, the young Danish ballerina Lucile Grahn, who excelled in *pirouettes*, then Carlotta Grisi, followed by Fanny Cerrito, an Italian dancer of uncommon speed and brilliance.

These and other ballerinas continually expanded the limits of ballet technique. They rivaled male dancers in the size of their leaps and the speed of their footwork. They danced more and more on the tips of their toes, an achievement requiring tremendous strength in soft slippers. A little darning around the point of the shoe, a little cotton batting inside, and ribbons tied tightly around the ankles offered the only assistance to Taglioni and others of her era. The delicately pale, unworldly romantic ballerina was, in fact, a far stronger technician than her robust, voluptuous eighteenth-century predecessor. For the first time in the history of Western theatrical dancing, females, now *en pointe*, replaced males as the dominant stage performers. However, two male dancer-choreographers of the period deserve special mention: Auguste Bournonville, developer of the Danish repertory, and Arthur Saint-Léon, creator of *Coppélia* and a system of dance notation.

Bournonville studied with Auguste Vestris, and through his many ballets still performed today by the Royal Danish Ballet, and by his documentation of ballet

Jules Perrot's plotless divertissement *Pas de Quatre* (1845) cleverly displayed the individual skills of four of the greatest ballerinas of the romantic period, shown here in the pose with which the ballet began and ended. Surrounding Marie Taglioni are Carlotta Grisi, Lucile Grahn, and Fanny Cerrito.

COURTESY OF THE DANCE COLLECTION, THE NEW YORK PUBLIC LIBRARY AT LINCOLN CENTER, ASTOR, LENOX AND TILDEN FOUNDATIONS.

technique in *Études chorégraphiques* (Copenhagen, 1861), Bournonville is responsible for keeping alive much of the French ballet tradition. His version of *La Sylphide*, not Taglioni's, is the one seen today. Bournonville should not be accused of plagiarism; adapting someone else's ballet without necessarily giving credit to the originator or using the original musical score was a common practice in both the eighteenth and nineteenth centuries.

Saint-Léon's international career was also typical of dancers and ballet masters of the time. He worked in London, St. Petersburg, Rome, Brussels, Milan, and Vienna, as well as his native Paris. Somehow he found time to publish, in 1852, a system of dance notation, *Sténochorégraphie.* Easy to decipher, his notation and descriptions give vivid examples of classroom exercises closely related to the earlier tradition described by Blasis and Théleur, including *grands pirouettes* and multiple beats.

Besides Elssler's *Cachucha*, the only other completely notated dances of the first half of the nineteenth century are the *Gavotte de Vestris*, an already famous duet by the time Théleur notated it, and a *pas de six* from *La Vivandière*, one of Saint-Léon's popular ballets and his only piece he succeeded in recording. Sad to say, most of the great romantic ballet repertory has been forgotten, and the rest has survived only through fallible memory. However, the works of another product of the era of romantic ballet, those of Marius Petipa, have enjoyed unusual longevity and deserve special attention in any ballet survey.

THE PETIPA YEARS

In the second half of the nineteenth century, the great opera houses of Europe relied more and more on spectacular vehicles tailored for the talents of a star ballerina. Smaller provincial theatres, unable to satisfy public taste for such elaborate fare, gradually ceased sponsoring new ballet productions, thus drying up a traditional source for inventive choreography. The lack of fine roles for male dancers and public preference for female dancers resulted in women taking leading male roles *en travestie.* The role of Franz in *Coppélia*, for instance, was originated by the shapely Eugénie Fiocre, a tradition for that ballet that continued well into this century.

London, once an ardent sponsor of the finest ballets at Her Majesty's Theatre, began to relegate dancing to divertissements during intervals between other acts at the Alhambra and Empire music halls. In Copenhagen, Bournonville managed to preserve the artistry of the romantic period, avoiding excesses he observed elsewhere: "Dancers have now run to technicalities and effects, choreography to decor, fountains and panoramas."[33] His comment referred in this instance to the Russian repertory of the 1870s, before it entered a period of brilliant successes that in many ways marked the glorious culmination of the romantic era.

The Russian theatre had long relied on foreign talent for its ballet. French ballet master Jean-Baptiste Landé was imported in 1734, and Charles LePicq followed fifty years later. Didelot came to St. Petersburg at the start of the nineteenth century, revolutionizing teaching methods and establishing the foundation of the Russian school. His work was continued by his fellow countrymen Perrot and Saint-Léon. Still another Frenchman, Marius Petipa, was to have the greatest effect. Arriving in St. Petersburg in 1847 at age twenty-five, he was to become *premier danseur* and then ballet master of the Imperial Ballet. By the end of his remarkable fifty-six-year career, Petipa had created close to sixty ballets and so nurtured native Russian talent that his adopted country, and in due time the world, was convinced that the very best in ballet meant Russian ballet.

A Petipa production meant evening-length ballets of several acts, fantastic stage effects, and fairy-tale plot related through pantomimic gestures by characters whose natures were revealed through their dances. Diversity during the long evening was achieved by alternating acts having naturalistic settings, which might include lively comic or folk dance–inspired passages, with acts having supernatural locations, perhaps a dream sequence with enchanted, winged creatures. Beautiful symmetry characterized Petipa ballet—groups of four, eight, thirty-two, or more lovely women moving in ingenious patterns. Dance passages often were repeated three times, then brought to an appropriately bravura finish. The hero and heroine usually performed only in the nobler, classical style, and their *pas de deux* was the highlight of any given act. With Petipa, the *grand pas de deux—adagio*, variations, and coda—reached a level of artistry that is still much admired, remaining technically challenging as well. Some Petipa repertory was preserved in a system of notation devised by Vladimir Stepanov and later used to mount the ballets in the West. One of these, *The Sleeping Beauty*, produced in 1890, was perhaps Petipa's crowning achievement. Its scenario was meticulously outlined by Petipa for Tchaikowsky, whose score is considered one of the finest.

It would be unfair to leave the impression that Marius Petipa singlehandedly made Russia the ballet capital of the world, for he had help from many sources. His talented but humble assistant, Lev Ivanov, was responsible for choreography of *The Nutcracker* and for Acts II and IV of *Swan Lake*, two other ballets with music by Tchaikowsky that probably are the most popular works associated with ballet from the 1890s. Christian Johannsen, a pupil of Bournonville who was already a leading dancer with the Imperial Ballet when Petipa first arrived, later become one of the finest teachers of its school. In the latter part of the century, the Imperial Theatre was host to a galaxy of Italian stars, products of the Blasis tradition of rigorous schooling. Among them were Virginia Zucchi and Pierina Legnani, whose amazing technique (including Legnani's sensational thirty-two *fouettés*) was carefully studied and then emulated by Russian dancers. Another technical wizard from Italy, Enrico Cecchetti, became an invaluable teacher in Russia before bringing his unique method of instruction to the West.

With the graduation of Olga Preobrajenska in 1889, and of Mathilde Kchessinska the following year, the Imperial Theatre School produced two native dancers as glorious as the foreign artists who had so long monopolized the Russian ballet spotlight. They were only the first of many. Imagine the excitement of classrooms where pupils such as Anna Pavlova, Tamara Karsavina, and Michel Fokine came from childhood on for their daily lessons. A class of perfection was established for such outstanding artists of the school. Nicolas Legat succeeded his master, Johannsen, as instructor, and accounts of his teaching can be found in *Heritage of a Ballet Master: Nicolas Legat,*[34] by one of his pupils, André Eglevsky, later a soloist with the New York City Ballet.

Ballet at the Imperial Theatre (renamed the Maryinsky; today known as the Kirov) was the pride of the czars, whose purse generously funded it. Productions at the lesser-renowned Bolshoi Theatre in Moscow grew in importance under the leadership of Alexander Gorsky.

By the end of the nineteenth century, dancers and audiences had grown accustomed to a kind of ballet ritual revolving around bravura technique. A slightly stiffer ballet slipper was developed that allowed the ballerinas to try more and more difficult steps on point. Male dancers regularly performed eight or more spins (*pirouettes*) and multiple crossings (*entrechats*) of the legs while in the air. Solo dances stopped the show, and the excitement was so great that even a ballerina's entrance was greeted with applause. Indeed she was an impressive sight, with diamonds sparkling from her head, ears, and neck. No matter what her role or the theme of the ballet, a ballerina wore jewels from her private collection (usually gifts from titled admirers) and a full-skirted, tight-waisted costume (*tutu*) that reached to just above her knees. Soloists were allowed to insert their favorite steps into the choreography; they danced along with the music but otherwise considered it an incidental element.

Noverre would have written a manifesto scolding such absurdities just as he did in his own time, almost a hundred and fifty years before. As it happened, a young Russian dancer and choreographer, Michel Fokine, picked up the pen in 1904 and urged the ballet administration to work for more harmonious productions in which music, decor, costume, and dance would blend in a meaningful way. He decried the gymnastics that had crept into ballet at the expense of a sensitive interpretation of a chosen theme. He believed a mood or story line should be understandable through the dance, rather than dependent on passages of pantomime.

Soon after, Isadora Duncan, a free-spirited American dancer, visited Russia and greatly impressed Fokine, Gorsky, and others with her expressivity, her sensitivity to music, and her revolutionary appearance—bare feet, unbound hair, and flowing Grecian tunic. While the Russians did not wish to emulate Duncan's contempt for the classical ballet, they believed innovative ideas like hers would bring freshness into the static situation in Russian theatres. But management did not approve of suggestions in this direction (Marius Petipa had retired by 1903, but traditions established during his reign continued). Subsequently a group of Russian artists, including Fokine, determined to bring ballet into the twentieth century, and to transport their ideas and talents out of Russia for the rest of the world to appreciate. It was a challenge, and it proved to be their glory.

THE DIAGHILEV BALLETS RUSSES

The one performance in all ballet history that most dancers wish they could have seen occurred in Paris on an evening in May 1909. It was the European debut of the Ballets Russes, the birth of a new era in ballet. Instead of one full-length ballet, the program consisted of several distinctly different offerings, each with its own dance style. The dancing seemed born of the music; the costumes of the moving figures blended into the decor of the stage—it was "total theatre," the dream of Michel Fokine brought to reality by a company of young Russians.

At the helm of this historic troupe was Serge Diaghilev, artistic director and impressario extraordinary. Though skilled in neither painting, music, nor dance, he had the capacity to discover and inspire the greatest talents in each of those areas, and he longed to prove the talents of his countrymen—to themselves and to a Europe that had heretofore considered Russia a rather barbaric land. Before the formation of the Ballets Russes, Diaghilev had brought Russian art to Paris galleries, Russian music to its concert halls, and finally a production of *Boris Godunov* to the Paris Opéra itself. The success of these ventures challenged him to test Paris with the outstanding stars of the Russian ballet in productions completely new to Europe.

Diaghilev knew the choreographic potential of Fokine, who was eager to have his ballets staged without the restrictions imposed by the Maryinsky management. The ballets that Diaghilev selected for the Paris season included *Le Pavillon d'Armide*, evoking the gracious style of the court of Louis XIV; *Cléopâtre*, a dramatic vision of ancient Egypt; *Les Sylphides*, a suite of dances in romantic style and costume; and the savage Polovtsian dances from the opera *Prince Igor*. Collaborations were started with St. Petersburg painters Alexandre Benois and Léon Bakst for sets and costumes. Igor Stravinsky was asked to arrange some of the Chopin music for *Les Sylphides*. The Russian theatres agreed to release Fokine and a number of other dancers to go with Diaghilev during the summer months when they were not working. No one has ever assembled a finer roster of dancers, some of whom became legends in their own lifetimes. Leading *danseur* was Vaslav Nijinsky, possessor of an incredible elevation, a magnetic stage personality, and an acting ability that matched his fabulous dance technique. Heading the list of ballerinas was Anna Pavlova, who seemed to epitomize the Fokine philosophy. She had an uncanny ability to use every part of her exquisite body to create a magical image of motion and stillness that seemed beyond the range of mere bones and muscles. For her, Fokine had created *The*

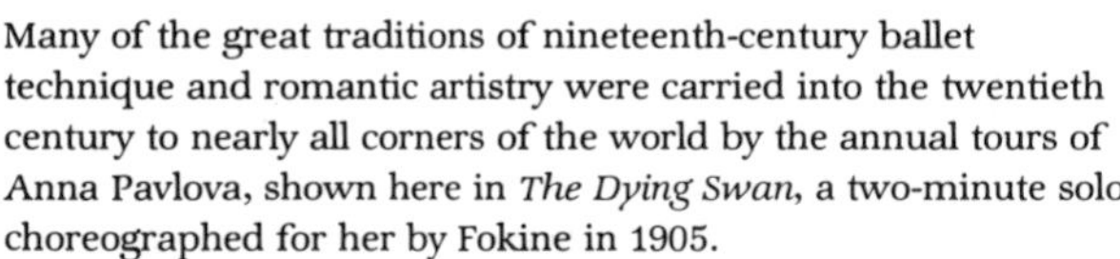

Many of the great traditions of nineteenth-century ballet technique and romantic artistry were carried into the twentieth century to nearly all corners of the world by the annual tours of Anna Pavlova, shown here in *The Dying Swan*, a two-minute solo choreographed for her by Fokine in 1905.

COURTESY OF THE DANCE COLLECTION, THE NEW YORK PUBLIC LIBRARY AT LINCOLN CENTER, ASTOR, LENOX AND TILDEN FOUNDATIONS.

Dying Swan, perhaps the finest dramatic ballet solo ever devised. Among the other stars of that first Paris season were Tamara Karsavina, Vera Fokina (wife of Michel Fokine), Adolph Bolm, and Mikhail Mordkin.

They set out on an unprecedented adventure, meticulously and extravagantly guided by Diaghilev, even to the redecoration of the Théâtre du Châtelet and the seating of the most attractive influential people for that first audience. The season was a triumph. Paris (where the *danseur* was known as a *porteur* because his main function was to lift the ballerina) was astounded by the virile dancing of the Russian men in *Prince Igor*. The bold colors used by Bakst for the decor of *Cléopâtre* were completely new to the Paris stage, as was the total harmony of costumes and sets created by Benois for *Le Pavillon d'Armide* and *Les Sylphides*. Paris was accustomed to a *corps de ballet* that served as little more than living scenery; the Russians instead presented an ensemble of fine dancers, in which each individual contributed to the overall effect. The versatility of all the ballerinas was admired, but Paris was captivated by the exotic beauty and dramatic skills of Ida Rubinstein as Cléopâtre.

As the Paris press trumpeted every aspect of the Ballets Russes, its distribution of praise had two monumental effects on the course of ballet history: It tempted Diaghilev to arrange future summer seasons for his ballet company in Europe, and it tempted Pavlova to strike out on her own. Having been offered other engagements outside Russia, she soon left both the Diaghilev company and the Maryinsky Theatre, eventually forming her own company. She became a kind of dance missionary, bringing ballet and her own unique artistry to practically every section of the globe. A whole generation of dancers, would-be dancers, and ballet fans emerged because they "had seen Pavlova." There were few masterpieces in her repertory other than Fokine's *Dying Swan*, but Pavlova, as dragonfly or snowflake or butterfly, infused even inferior choreography and insipid music with a special magic.

The years from 1909 to 1913 marked a period of notable success for all concerned. Diaghilev formed a permanent company, one completely independent from the Russian theatres. The prolific Fokine created *Schéhérazade, The Firebird, Carnaval, Specter of the Rose, Daphnis and Chloë, Petrouchka,* and eight other ballets of lesser fame. Igor Stravinsky, commissioned to compose music for *The Firebird,* became famous as a result and began his close collaboration with the Diaghilev Ballet. The costumes designed by Léon Bakst for *Schéhérazade* launched a wave of semioriental fashion for Parisian women.

The dancers were continually challenged by new and different roles. With the exit of Pavlova, Karsavina became the leading ballerina. Nijinsky revealed his unique gifts as a choreographer. His ballets, notably *Afternoon of a Faun* and *The Rite of Spring,* seemed a denial of classical ballet; their angular, "primitive" movements and rhythmic motivation anticipated a vocabulary later developed by such modern dancers as Mary Wigman and Martha Graham.

Much to Diaghilev's pleasure, his troupe produced one novel ballet after another, although not all were successful with the public and the press. Then came 1914 and World War I. In spite of the chaos of the times, Diaghilev determined to continue his company. Around a newly discovered choreographic talent, Leonide Massine, a new repertory began to take shape. Promising young dancers were recruited: Stanislas Idzikowski and Leon Woizikowski from Poland and Vera Nemtchinova from Moscow. An English dancer, Hilda Munnings, joined the company and was renamed Lydia Sokolova. Cecchetti was engaged to guide these and other young talents in daily classes of strict technique. His method of instruction, including set *adagio* and *allegro* sequences for each day of the week, was compiled in *A Manual of the Theory and Practice of Classical Theatrical Dancing* (London, 1922).[35] Besides Bakst and Stravinsky, there were Michel Larionov, painter, and Ernest Ansermet, conductor. Diaghilev had again assembled a group of geniuses, and the Ballets Russes continued, very like a tiny, independent kingdom of art in the midst of a world at war.

Massine produced several popular ballets in quick succession: *The Good-Humored Ladies, La Boutique Fantasque,* and *The Three-Cornered Hat.* His most startling effort was the surrealist ballet *Parade,* with decor and costumes by Picasso. In later years the choreographic skills of Bronislava Nijinska (sister of Vaslav) and George Balanchine (a 1924 defector from the Soviet Union) were encouraged. Composers who worked with the company included Satie, Poulenc, Milhaud, de Falla, Prokofiev, Ravel, Debussy, and, of course, Stravinsky. In 1928, Stravinsky and Balanchine began a collaboration that extended more than forty years. An early effort, *Apollon Musagète* (now known simply as *Apollo*), introduced a "neoclassical" style in which academic ballet training served as a base for stunning technical innovation—for example, acrobatic lifts and leaps, turns with the body close to the floor, and movements and poses done on point but with sharply bent knees.

The Diaghilev stage served as an inviting canvas for such painters as Braque, Picasso, Derain, and Rouault. The roster of dancers was ever-changing and ever-exciting. Books have been written about many of them, but all deserve at least mention in any historical account. Space limits us merely to listing a few additional names: Spessivtzeva, Lopokova, Dolin, Danilova, Markova, Egorova, Nikitina, Doubrovska, Lifar.

They lived a nomadic and precarious existence, these members of the first great ballet company without backing from a state or royal treasury. Home became Monte Carlo for rehearsal periods and an annual season, but the company existed only from one season to the next, dependent on bookings in Europe, South America, and the United States, on alliances with influential impressarios of opera houses, and on the generosity of wealthy patrons; somehow necessary financing was always secured just in time. For twenty years the Ballets Russes led the world to a new appreciation of ballet. But it was Diaghilev's company, and with his death in 1929 the organization collapsed, the dancers scattered, and an era ended.

BALLET AFTER DIAGHILEV

The vision that Diaghilev had was too strong to die completely with him. During the 1930s there emerged a series of companies whose names incorporated the magic box-office words "Ballet Russe" or "Monte Carlo" and whose repertories preserved many of the great ballets from the Diaghilev years. Massine continued to create remarkable ballets, some to symphonic scores, his lighter works including *Gaité Parisienne* and *Capriccio Espagnol.* The companies included many of the stars from the Diaghilev ballet plus an international list of new talents, such as Igor Youskevitch, Frederic Franklin, George Zoritch, André Eglevsky, Mia Slavinska, and the "baby ballerinas" Toumanova, Riabouchinska, and Baronova.

The constant touring of these companies during the 1930s and 1940s produced a new generation of ballet fans. England and the United States were

Some of the innovative repertory from Diaghilev's Ballets Russes has survived through revivals by subsequent companies. George Zoritch, soloist with Ballet Russe de Monte Carlo and Grand Ballet du Marquis de Cuevas, is pictured here in Fokine's *Le Spectre de la Rose* ("The Spirit of the Rose") created for Nijinsky in 1911.

PHOTO: SERGE LIDO.

especially receptive, and serious efforts were made to encourage native talent and establish permanent companies in those countries. No state support for such projects existed in either England or the United States, but by the great determination and dedication of a few persons, companies were formed and, more important, ballet schools were established.

In 1920 Marie Rambert founded a school and began the groundwork for what became Ballet Rambert, now Britain's oldest dance company. Always providing an atmosphere for experimentation, the company gave early choreographic opportunities to Frederick Ashton, Agnes De Mille, and Antony Tudor. Since 1966 it has been primarily a modern dance troupe, a reorganization fully endorsed by Rambert, who as a girl had studied eurhythmics, a system of translating musical rhythms into body movements. She used these skills to coach Nijinsky, at Diaghilev's suggestion, in preparation for Stravinsky's challenging score for *Rite of Spring*.

Another grand dream was conceived and carried out by Ninette de Valois, a former student of Cecchetti and dancer with the Diaghilev company. From her London studio, founded in 1926, emerged a company known as the Vic-Wells, then as the Sadler's Wells Ballet when it moved to the theatre by that name. The de Valois policy of carefully recreating nineteenth-century classics was epitomized by the revival of the original Petipa version of *Sleeping Beauty*, staged by former Maryinsky dancer Nicholas Sergeyev from the Stepanov notation. It became the company's signature piece, used in a gala performance after World War II for the reopening of the Royal Opera House at Covent Garden, the company's new home, and for its first triumphant New York season in 1949. The role of Princess Aurora in the ballet has been indelibly associated with Margot Fonteyn, a product of the school who became one of the world's truly exquisite ballerinas. The company was awarded a royal charter in 1956, thus becoming the Royal Ballet and fulfilling the de Valois dream. Principal choreographer Ashton, and later Kenneth MacMillan, built a balanced repertory of contemporary ballets and new productions of the classics.

Another British institution begun in the 1920s deserves mention in a ballet textbook history: the Royal Academy of Dancing (RAD). Its initial purpose was to raise the artistic level of dancing and to improve teaching methods in Britain. Its first syllabus, written by Edouard Espinosa, reflected his French training, but also the Italian, Danish, Russian, and English traditions of the other founding members. Annual examinations, now worldwide, and teachers' training courses continue the ideals of the Academy.

THE AMERICAN SCENE

Across the Atlantic, early twentieth-century performing outlets for American dancers included musical revues, vaudeville tours, and occasional concerts by small troupes from local studios—not unlike the dance opportunities in Britain at the time. Opera companies in New York, and later in San Francisco and Chicago, maintained a European repertory and performance model in which, at most, dance was an incidental divertissement. However, a young Harvard graduate, Lincoln Kirstein, envisioned an American ballet company and fortunately had the financial means to implement his plans, for there was no governmental help, not even, as in most countries, a secretary or minister for the arts. Impressed with the neoclassical choreography of George Balanchine during the last years of the Diaghilev company, Kirstein invited the young choreographer to the United States to found a company. Balanchine's famous reply, "But first, a school," resulted in the establishment of the School of American Ballet. In that same year, 1934, Balanchine devised his first American ballet, *Serenade* (to Tchaikowsky's Serenade for String Orchestra), as a study in performance technique for his students. The school and that particular ballet have flourished to this day, although the company had a rocky start. First called the American Ballet, it

The dynamic partnership of Margot Fonteyn and Rudolf Nureyev, shown here in the "Black Swan" *pas de deux* from Petipa and Ivanov's *Le Lac des Cygnes* ("Swan Lake," 1895) combined the English and Russian ballet traditions to the delight of Western audiences during the 1960s.

PHOTO: JUDY CAMERON.

operated for a short period as the resident company for the Metropolitan Opera, but Balanchine's disregard for simple, traditional operatic dances upset the directors, singers, and conservative audience and soon finished off the relationship. After periods of little activity and reorganization with another Kirstein group, Ballet Caravan, the company finally in 1948 found a performing home, the New York City Center, and a new name, the New York City Ballet (NYCB).

The company repertory and style have always been dominated by Balanchine, even though Jerome Robbins, an American dancer-choreographer, was added as an associate director. In spite of his Maryinsky background, Balanchine choreographed only a few full-length ballets—*Jewels, Don Quixote, A Midsummer Night's Dream,* and a perenially popular version of *The Nutcracker.* Instead, he usually followed the Diaghilev formula of three or four short ballets on each program. But unlike most ballets from the Diaghilev years, the Balanchine selections seldom have a story line or elaborate decor. Music, often an intricate score from Stravinsky, was the catalyst for Balanchine's "pure dance" ballets, usually set on a bare stage and performed with incredible speed and stamina by dancers (most of whom trained in the company school) dressed in tights, leotards, or simple tunics.

Balanchine's 1957 ballet *Agon* packed an unprecedented amount of movement into only twenty minutes. Classical technique was stretched and explored as it never had been before. The complexities of Stravinsky's rhythms and twelve-tone style were matched by Balanchine's twelve disciplined dancers. It was a turning point for ballet, as the Balanchine-Stravinsky *Apollo* had been almost thirty years before.

The company seldom tours, enjoying lengthy seasons and the stability of a home base, now at New York's handsome Lincoln Center for the Performing Arts. City Ballet, as it is familiarly known, has produced many fine male dancers, such as Edward Villella, Jacques d'Amboise, and Arthur Mitchell. But, to most minds, the "Balanchine dancer" is typified by such streamlined ballerinas as Diana Adams, Tanaquil LeClerq, and Maria Tallchief; later, Allegra Kent, Suzanne Farrell, and Patricia McBride; and more recently, Kyra Nichols and Darci Kistler, who at age eighteen became the youngest principal dancer in the company's history. All have performed with pistonlike point work and limber, over-the-head extensions, technical attributes now expected by most companies, many of whom have added Balanchine ballets to their repertories. Danish-trained principal dancer Peter Martins has gained recent critical acclaim for his choreography, building on the Balanchine model but promising to carve out a distinctive style of his own. In 1983 George Balanchine died, and Martins and Robbins were given responsibility for the operation of the company.

American Ballet Theatre (ABT) has followed quite a different path. Founded by Lucia Chase and Richard Pleasant, the company, until 1957 known simply as Ballet Theatre, has, from its opening season in 1940, been a kind of touring library of ballet. Its repertory tries to remain as strong in revived or revised classics as it is in works of established contemporary choreographers, both

A *pas de deux* from the Balanchine/Stravinsky collaboration *Agon* ("Contest," 1957) is pictured as performed by its original New York City Ballet cast, Arthur Mitchell and Diana Adams. This plotless ballet, with its revealing classroom dress and its exploration of the technical range and complexity possible within the ballet medium, has had great impact on subsequent productions and perhaps even on ballet training.

PHOTO: MARTHA SWOPE.

American and foreign, and in the experimental attempts of newcomers. Opportunities given to Agnes De Mille, Jerome Robbins, Michael Kidd, and Herbert Ross resulted in exciting, often-masterful ballets.

At the invitation of Ballet Theatre, Antony Tudor came to America from England and brought a new dimension for ballet. It has been called a psychological element, for Tudor deals with the motivations and emotions of ordinary people—their hopes, their struggles, their foibles—replacing the stylized poses of classical technique with natural gestures. Rejecting dance-for-dance's-sake, he offers instead a continuous flow of movement that carries the action of ballet to its inevitable conclusion. Tudor requires that his dancers be fine actors as well as strong technicians—a challenge met especially well by Nora Kaye, Hugh Laing, and Sallie Wilson. In 1942, Ballet Theatre produced Tudor's *Pillar of Fire,* the story of Hagar, who, fearful that she will be a spinster like her older sister, has an affair with a young man and then later finds forgiveness and peace with the one she had loved earlier. *Pillar of Fire* became an immediate success, assuring a prominent place for the ballet with a psychological theme.

Offering perhaps the most varied repertory of any company in the world (as many as sixty ballets by thirty different choreographers in a single season) and promoting guest artists, ABT has long attracted ballet superstars, from Alicia Alonso (Cuba) to Erik Bruhn (Denmark), and more recently Natalia Makarova (Soviet Union). Another Soviet expatriate, Mikhail Baryshnikov, joined Makarova as a member of the company, becoming artistic director in 1980. Baryshnikov's own high level of virtuosity has given a new boost to traditional ballet roles and to the technique itself. Dance critic Arlene Croce expresses it well:

> For Baryshnikov, a double *pirouette* or air turn is a linking step, and preparations barely exist. . . . He also performs invented steps. One is a turning *jeté* in which, at the last second, he changes the foot he's going to land on and his legs flash past each other in the air. . . . Baryshnikov's promise lies not in novel steps but in his power to push classical steps to a new extreme in logic, a new density of interest. He is a modern classical dancer.[36]

BALLET ECLECTICISM

Early in the twentieth century some American dancers believed the codified technique and Russo-European traditions of ballet were an inappropriate and inadequate means of expression for their country and their time. Such persons were called "modern" dancers because, following the inspiration of Isadora Duncan, they broke with all traditional forms in an effort to devise a more natural dance expression.

A school and company called Denishawn were established in Los Angeles in 1915 by two pioneers of the new dance, Ruth St. Denis and her husband Ted Shawn. Oddly enough, St. Denis found many of her movement themes in religious dances of the Orient. Shawn, on the other hand, filled his dances with

Americana, using subjects and styles especially suited to the male dancer—American Indians, laborers, farmers, athletes. From the amalgam that was the Denishawn group came Martha Graham, Doris Humphrey, and Charles Weidman, all of whom founded companies of their own and eventually evolved movement principles on which new dance techniques were built.

Their influence was felt in ballet circles, where choreographers began to look for subject matter from their native land and movements that would appropriately illustrate those themes. Among the first successful ballets of this type were *Filling Station* by Lew Christensen and *Billy the Kid* by Eugene Loring, both produced in 1938 by Ballet Caravan. The Wild West was the inspiration of another popular work a few years later, *Rodeo*, by Agnes De Mille. Like De Mille, Jerome Robbins brought to ballet choreography a varied background—ballet, modern, jazz, tap—that he brilliantly wove into a little masterpiece, *Fancy Free*, the saga of three sailors on leave in Manhattan, set to a new jazz score by Leonard Bernstein in 1944.

New York became the dance capital of the United States, but ballet activity had spread from coast to coast. The San Francisco Ballet celebrated its fiftieth anniversary in 1983, making it the oldest company in the country. Emerging as a separate entity from the San Francisco Opera, the company, under the leadership of William Christensen, offered the first full-length production of *Swan Lake* staged by an American. Other companies were established in the 1930s in Chicago (by Ruth Page and Bentley Stone) and in Philadelphia (by Catherine Littlefield). National interest in ballet was furthered during tours by newly organized Ballets Russes—various companies led by René Blum, Colonel Wassili de Basil, and Sergei Denham. Today the Boston Ballet, Pennsylvania Ballet, Ballet West (in Salt Lake City), and the Houston Ballet are some of the fully professional companies in the United States.

The costs of maintaining such companies are overwhelming to all but the most stouthearted and determined directors. Robert Joffrey is an outstanding example of success at great odds. Beginning in 1954 with six dancers, the Robert Joffrey Ballet toured in a station wagon, presenting a repertory of four Joffrey works, performed in borrowed costumes to taped music. By the 1960s, the company had twenty dancers, a ten-piece orchestra, and funding from private foundations. Continuing to expand during the next twenty years, it came to share popularity ranking with NYCB and ABT. Joffrey expects his dancers to perform as individuals in ballets of many diverse styles and periods, whether composed by the prolific assistant director, Gerald Arpino, or by visiting artists from the modern dance tradition, such as Twyla Tharp and Laura Dean. Revivals from the Diaghilev era and from Kurt Jooss's expressionistic European ballets of the 1930s have added to the eclectic nature of the repertory. High performance standards are maintained through the company school (American Dance Center in New York City) and by an apprentice company, the Joffrey II Dancers. A pioneering effort was the recent establishment of a joint base of

Nigel Courtney seems to fly across stage as Ariel in *The Tempest,* a full-length ballet based on Shakespeare's play. Created in 1980 for the San Francisco Ballet by co-director Michael Smuin, the ballet transferred successfully to the television screen for the *Dance in America* series.

PHOTO:RUDI LEGNAME.

The Joffrey Ballet repertory includes several works created for the company by modern dance choreographers. In 1982 Laura Dean composed both the movement and music for *Fire,* here performed by Patricia Brown and Luis Perez.

PHOTO: HERBERT MIGDOLL.

operations—New York and Los Angeles—whereby the Joffrey Ballet became the first two-city company.

The Dance Theatre of Harlem, the Eliot Feld Ballet, and the Los Angeles Ballet are a few of the other companies that manage to survive in an unpredictable field. But many a creative entrepreneur has had to be satisfied with establishing a small concert group whose members support themselves by means other than performing—all clearly professionals in every sense except that they do not receive a salary commensurate with the minimum required by the American Guild of Musical Artists (AGMA), the union for dancers in ballet, modern companies, or opera. Other choreographers and dancers, finding the Broadway stage, films, and television more reliable for earning a decent wage, have helped to make the musical comedy perhaps America's greatest contribution to the theatre and to create new audiences by introducing dance to the television screen. The vast possibilities of televised dance are yet to be explored by choreographers.

Until recently, most companies—large or small, professional or semiprofessional—made a go of it or not according to the Diaghilev method: Tour a lot and try to make up deficits by soliciting gifts from wealthy patrons. Even this usually failed to bring in enough money, and most director-choreographers saved themselves and their companies by teaching.

Gradually, large foundations have been attracted to dance. Enormous grants were given by the Ford Foundation, principally to the New York City Ballet, and the Rothschild Foundation has supported Martha Graham for years. This is a happy situation for the "haves" but a frustrating one for the "have-nots." Finally, aid began to come from government through the National Endowment for the Arts and from state arts councils, though always vulnerable to economic trends and priorities set by new administrations.

While professional dancers are enjoying somewhat greater security and prestige, amateur dancers are in the midst of an unprecedented local and regional dance boom. The civic ballet movement began in Atlanta in 1941 under the inspiration of Dorothy Alexander. Thirty years later the *Dance Magazine Directory of Dance Attractions* listed 150 civic companies. In 1983, 156 companies belonged to the National Association for Regional Ballet (NARB), an organization (also begun by Alexander) that promotes high performing and teaching standards through mutual communication, sharing of membership resources, and five regional performance festivals each year.

Fine professional (high standards/serious students) ballet schools are found in almost all large cities, and practically every phone book in the country lists at least one ballet studio in its yellow pages. During the 1960s and 1970s, colleges and universities eagerly added ballet courses to dance curricula that formerly encouraged only modern dance on campuses. Professional dancers are being attracted to university faculties, where it is becoming less and less the case of one college-trained teacher turning out another college-trained teacher. The professional dance world and the academic dance world are profiting from the exchange, as ballet and modern dance are benefiting from mutual attractions and understandings. No longer can a modern dancer ignore ballet technique, nor can a ballet dancer remain "untainted" by other dance forms.

The United States enjoys a prominence in the current jet age of dance. A good New York review is as prized as a Paris review once was. Companies from far shores come for a New York season and often a tour of other cities. The Bolshoi was perhaps the most eagerly awaited visitor, making an enormously successful New York debut in 1959. Its prima ballerina, Galina Ulanova, had trained with Agrippina Vaganova in her method that now is the basis for ballet education in Eastern Bloc countries. Vaganova's 1934 textbook *Basic Principles of Classical Ballet*[37] shows her amalgam of the French and Italian traditions now absorbed into Russian teaching. In 1959, American audiences were stunned by Bolshoi virtuosity, especially the elevation and strength of its male dancers, who could carry their partners overhead in effortless lifts supported by only one hand. Since then, regular exchanges have taken place between United States and Soviet Union dance attractions, some not always sanctioned by the Soviets, beginning with the 1962 defection by Kirov dancer Rudolf Nureyev. Two interesting by-products of this exchange, whether official or not, seemingly have been the greater appreciation of male dancing in the West and a slimmer ballet silhouette for dancers in the East.

The Royal Winnipeg Ballet and the National Ballet of Canada come south regularly. South African–born John Cranko brought his exciting company from Stuttgart, performing full-length versions of *Romeo and Juliet*, *The Taming of the Shrew*, and *Eugene Onegin*. A small part of the United States has seen the Ballets of the Twentieth Century, a highly controversial company from Belgium, headed by Maurice Béjart, a Frenchman whose ideas of total theatre speak with particular effectiveness to today's youth. Other welcome visitors include the Royal Danish Ballet, with its well-preserved and increasingly popular Bournonville repertory, and the perennial favorite, Britain's Royal Ballet.

It is the age of the guest artist, who can jet from capital to capital for one-night appearances and a hefty check. Good choreographers are always in demand, crisscrossing the globe from one assignment to another. Although ballet developed in the Western world, it is now also a part of the rich dance culture of Japan and China. International ballet competitions rotate annually between Tokyo, Moscow, Varna, and Jackson, Mississippi.

It seems that ballet has come a very long way from its early days as royal entertainment in the court of Louis XIV. But was it really so long ago? To trace one dancer's heritage, we can look, for example, at a contemporary ballerina Sallie Wilson. She studied with Margaret Craske, who was a pupil of Enrico Cecchetti. Cecchetti's teacher was Giovanni Lepri, a disciple of Blasis, who in turn had worked with Dauberval. Dauberval was Noverre's pupil. Noverre trained with Dupré, who succeeded Pécour and Beauchamps as ballet master at the Paris Opéra. Beauchamps was choreographer for Louis XIV. That is a span of only ten ballet generations. The ballet family tree has many branches, but it is not so very tall after all, and every ballet dancer today can connect somewhere to one of those branches. Even though ballet roots go very deep (some like to say back to ritual dances of ancient cultures), its fascinating/exasperating, logical/unnatural, tender/provocative, balanced/venturesome dance technique has a relatively brief history.

And it is a highly personal history. One pair of feet has demonstrated for another pair, one hand has guided another body, one voice has encouraged another soul, one set of muscles has remembered what a mind may have forgotten. Ballet has not been, cannot be, transmitted alone from book or machine. It is an experience that must be lived. Ten generations have so lived it, studied it, performed it, taught it, redirected it. We can look forward to more.

NOTES

1. The Domenico manuscript is in the Bibliothèque Nationale, Paris. *Saltare* was a term implying pantomime or representative dance by professional performers; the term came to mean jumping or leaping. *Chorea* was a term later identified with *carole*, line or closed-circle dances with participants holding hands; these dances could be stately and stepped or lively with hops. These and other early dance terms are discussed by Ingrid Brainard in "Dance of the Middle Ages and Early Renaissance," in *The New Grove Dictionary of Music and Musicians*, vol. 5 (London: MacMillan, 1980), 180–85.
2. Ingrid Brainard, "Domenico da Piacenza," in *The New Grove Dictionary of Music and Musicians*, vol. 5 (London: MacMillan, 1980), 332–33.
3. Plato, *The Laws*, VII, 814, in *The Dialogues of Plato*, trans. B. Jowett (Oxford, 1953), 383.
4. First established at the University of Wisconsin in Madison by Margaret H'Doubler in 1921.
5. Quintilian, *Institutio oratorio*, 11.3.88, trans. Frank W. D. Ries in "Roman Pantomime: Practice and Politics," *Dance Scope* 12 (Fall/Winter 1977–78): 40.
6. Clement of Alexandria, referring to a hymn in the Apocryphal Acts of St. John. Quoted in Kathy Meyer-Baer, *Music of the Spheres and the Dance of Death* (Princeton, N.J.: Princeton University Press, 1970), 35–36.
7. See transcription and translation by W. L. Smolden, *Planctus Mariae* (Oxford, England: Oxford University Press, n.d.).
8. Régine Kunzle, "In Search of L'Académie Royale de Danse," *York Dance Review* 7 (Spring 1978): 7.
9. *Ibid.*, 8.
10. *Ibid.*
11. Quoted in "Fifteenth- and Early Sixteenth-Century Court Dances," in *Institute of Court Dances of the Renaissance and Baroque Periods*, ed. Juana de Laban (New York: Dance Notation Bureau, 1972), 4.
12. *Pavana*, an adjective meaning "of Padua," implies that the dance took its name from that town. Some scholars believe the dance term (also *pavan, pavane*) derives from *pavón* (Spanish for peacock), indicating a relationship between the dignified, yet colorful dance and the elegant spread of a peacock's tail. *Gagliarda* (also *galliard, gaillarde*) means "vigorous, robust." *Saltarello*, or "little hop," is a dance form sometimes called *pas de brabant* or *alta danza*. *Canario* (also canary, *canarie*) is thought to be a dance form from the Canary Islands introduced to Spain in the sixteenth century and thence to the rest of the Continent.

13. Thoinot Arbeau, *Orchesography* (Langres, 1589), trans. Mary Stewart Evans, ed. Julia Sutton (New York: Dover, 1967), 81.
14. Quoted in *Le Balet Comique de la Royne*, 1581, trans. Carol and Lander MacClintock (American Institute of Musicology, 1971), 33.
15. *Ibid.*, 90–91.
16. James Miller, "The Philosophical Background of Renaissance Dance," *York Dance Review* 51 (Spring 1976): 3.
17. Quoted in Régine Kunzle, "Pierre Beauchamps: The Illustrious Unknown Choreographer: Part II," *Dance Scope*, (Fall/Winter 1974–75), 31.
18. *Ibid.*, 36.
19. Pierre Rameau, *The Dancing Master* (Paris, 1725), trans. Cyril W. Beaumont (New York: Dance Horizons, 1970), 5.
20. Joan Wildeblood, *The Polite World* (London: Davis-Poynter, 1973), 94.
21. Rameau (see Note 19) provides the most accessible information.
22. Exact translations and/or derivations of names of dances are often impossible to make and sometimes shed little light on the dance form itself. For instance, the late seventeenth–early eighteenth-century *courante* was majestic and grave, unlike the livelier *coranto* or *corrente* forms of the preceding era. The terms, however, can be translated as "running or flowing." Some scholars suggest the name *minuet* or *menuet* may have derived from the French "*menu*" (slender, small), perhaps referring to the small steps of the dance.
23. Quoted in Selma Jeanne Cohen, ed., *Dance as a Theatre Art* (New York: Dodd, Mead, 1974), 51.
24. Quoted in Lincoln Kirstein, *Dance: A Short History of Classic Theatrical Dancing* (New York: Dance Horizons, 1969), 209.
25. Jean Georges Noverre, *Letters on Dancing and Ballets*, trans. Cyril W. Beaumont (New York: Dance Horizons, 1968), 29, 99.
26. *Ibid.*, 117.
27. *Ibid.*, 99.
28. Quoted in Kirstein (see Note 23), 236.
29. Jack Anderson, *Dance* (New York: Newsweek Books, 1979), 46.
30. Translation by Mary Stewart Evans (New York: Dover, 1968).
31. *Ibid.*, 46.
32. *Théorie de la gymnastique de la dance théatrale* (Paris, 1859). Translated excerpts in Cohen (see Note 23), 71–77.
33. Quoted in Joan Lawson, *The History of Ballet and Its Makers* (London: Dance Books, 1973), 76.
34. (New York: Dance Horizons, 1977).
35. Cyril W. Beaumont and Stanislas Idzikowski, *A Manual of the Theory and Practice of Classical Theatrical Dancing* (New York: Dover, 1975).
36. Arlene Croce, "Mikhail Baryshnikov," in *The Dance Anthology*, ed. Cobbett Steinberg, (New York: New American Library, 1980), 121–22.
37. First published in Leningrad, Vaganova's book has been translated by Anatole Chujoy and republished by Dover (New York, 1969).

CHAPTER 2
THE BALLET CLASS

Technique classes six days a week are expected of students preparing for a professional career in ballet, but two or three classes per week may be more realistic for the adult beginner who has a different dance goal in mind. However, the benefits of the daily ballet class regimen are hard to deny, especially in view of the fact that muscles do not retain their stretch or strength. It is sobering to realize that within twenty-four hours after activity ceases, atrophy begins.

The necessary elements of any ballet class—the teacher, the studio, the student, the music, the vocabulary—and the first procedures of the lesson are the subjects of this chapter.

THE TEACHER

Most important to a ballet class is a well-qualified teacher. Indeed, all ballet artists credit their success to one or more great teachers with whom they have studied. These teachers most probably had been dancers themselves at one time, an important consideration for students bent on a professional dance career. An often-heard maxim, "Great dancers aren't always great teachers," is true enough, but a gifted teacher (usually with experience as a performer and some knowledge of classical ballet repertory) seems to be in the background of every great dancer.

The teacher of a beginning class for adults need not be a retired *prima ballerina* or *premier danseur* with firsthand acquaintance of famous ballet roles, but she or he should have a sound knowledge of ballet technique and an understanding of human anatomy. The instrument being trained is the human body; the teacher's job is, therefore, a complex and responsible one.

Knowing and showing the steps is not enough, especially for beginning classes. An exercise needs to be "broken down" into basic movements that must be mastered before the complete step is attempted. These slow, elementary exercises may seem totally unrelated to the brilliant footwork of dancers seen on stage and screen. Those serene artists show no signs of effort, sweat, or fatigue, but a visit backstage at a performance or to a professional class will quickly dispel the vision of effortless motion. To dance is to work, and to work very hard. It is the teacher's job to guide that work soundly, and the good teacher can often make it exciting and enjoyable.

Teaching methods and manners vary. One teacher may be "dressed out" in practice clothes like the rest of the class; another may wear street clothes and shoes. One instructor may demonstrate every exercise; another will remain seated throughout the lesson. A teacher's voice may be loud, accompanied by hand-clapping or stick-tapping, or it may be soft, as though only two persons were in the studio. Many teachers employ a variety of styles and resort to a number of ways of reaching the students—serious, joking, angry, anecdotal.

Correction and criticism are basic ingredients to instruction, and a good teacher knows when and how to give them to the beginner as well as to the advanced dancer. Basically there are two kinds of correction—that given to the entire class, and that given to an individual. Take heed of both! A soloist with a famous company has said that she always listened to a class correction as though it were said to her personally. When an individual correction is given, it should not be received as an embarrassing insult, and one hopes it was not offered in such a manner. Most teachers have a genuine interest in the progress of their pupils and a true dedication to ballet. A correction is considered an aid to progress, and the teacher is likely to lose interest in the student who ignores or systematically forgets criticism. If corrections apply to a serious structural problem and are still ignored, the student may be asked to withdraw from the class. Ballet technique is a powerful tool for building strong bodies, but when done incorrectly it is equally powerful in damaging them. The teacher of a beginning class for adults should not expect the technical perfection of a younger student enrolled in a professional ballet school. Neither should the adult who enrolls in a ballet class expect to float randomly around the room as music plays somewhere in the background.

Ballet's aristocratic heritage from royal courts has continued a certain formalism in manners as well as style. Thus, in class a certain politeness prevails, and the ballet teacher may expect to be addressed as Miss, Madame, or Mr. Such-and-Such even though some students in the class may be older than the teacher or on a first-name basis outside of class. Although this procedure may sound austere, it does not detract from the teacher's availability for answering serious questions and listening to individual problems. Adult classes offer both teacher and students the opportunity to discuss artistic and historical matters as well as technical concerns of ballet. The classroom should be a place to ask as well as to listen.

THE STUDIO

The ballet classroom is an unpretentious place, for the needs of the class are simple, though specific. Typically the room is fairly large, often approximating the rectangular shape and size of a stage. A wooden floor is essential. Dancers prefer it to be "raised" (the boards resting on joists, or supports) so as to allow a certain give under the weight of the body. This slight cushioning effect helps to reduce fatigue and to prevent injuries that can occur from dancing on a concrete floor. The raised floor usually is made of hardwood with its surface smooth, free of holes, but not slick. The sight of a shiny, gymnasium-type floor sends shudders through a ballet dancer, who much prefers an unwaxed, unvarnished floor kept clean by water only. Soap leaves a film, making the wood slippery, and any hint of its use sends the dancer in search of a rosin box. Rosin, which contains an adhesive substance, can be purchased in powder or crystal form. It is put into a box large enough for the dancer to step into, grinding the rosin into the soles of the ballet shoes. Many teachers dislike the use of rosin, and certainly it should never be used as a crutch to help hold a turnout in fifth position! If a floor is very slippery and rosin is not available, sometimes water-soaked paper towels can be placed at the edge of the studio for dampening shoes. A once-familiar sight before ballet class was the teacher sprinkling the floor with a watering can to prevent a slippery surface.

Every ballet studio contains *barres*, which are long railings made of wood or metal pipes, either attached to the walls or supported from the floor. A studio may also contain portable *barres*. Whether permanent or portable, they have to be steady, offering the student a secure place to begin the lesson. The average height of the *barre* from the floor is three feet, six inches, but obviously some adjustment can be made for the very short or very tall person. (See page 62 for further discussion of the relationship of the *barre* and the student.)

Usually at least one wall of the studio contains a mirror. Often one entire wall is covered by mirrors and designated the "front" of the room because the dancers face that wall when they leave the *barre* to do center work. The mirror allows the dancer to check instantly the correctness of a position or movement, but it can turn into another crutch, especially for the beginner. Students can become so accustomed to dancing before their own images that facing a non-mirrored wall leaves them at a loss. (This loss is nothing, however, compared with that felt by the dancer, trained and rehearsed in a mirrored studio, who first sets foot on a stage and faces, not mirrors, but the blackness of the auditorium.) Focusing on the mirror can often distort a position and actually make some movements more difficult (especially turns). A teacher is wise to change, at least occasionally, the "front" of the room to a nonmirrored wall.

A studio needs to be well ventilated but not drafty, and sufficiently warm to allow the muscles of the body to work easily. Few ballet facilities are luxurious, many are barely adequate, and some are depressingly dingy. But the art of ballet seems to transcend these surroundings as it passes from the careful teacher to the hard-working students, for ballet is not contained within the walls of the studio but within the body, mind, and spirit of the dancers.

THE STUDENT

Enrollment in a beginning ballet class should—but often does not—depend on permission of the instructor after a personal interview. This is particularly important for the admission of a child into a rigorous training program for professional ballet. Although the aspiration of an adult beginner is usually quite different, still it is important for the teacher to know whether the student has any physical handicaps. Of particular concern are problems of the heart, spine, knees, or feet. These may not preclude ballet study, but they may temper the way it is done.

CLOTHING

Students admitted into a beginning ballet class will need certain equipment: tights, leotard, soft ballet shoes. It is wise to check with the instructor for the preferred style and color of such items before purchasing them. In a college or university dance course, instructions about equipment often are given at the first class meeting.

Classroom dress for a woman means tights (usually pink), covering the body from feet to waist, and leotard (often black) worn over the tights from the hips to the shoulders. These practice clothes are made of a stretchable material that can be worn skintight and at the same time allow full freedom of movement with the outline of the body seen clearly. This exposure is often an unnerving experience for the beginner, but it is vital for the teacher, who is concerned with correct placement and movement of the body. Actually, tights and leotard are much less revealing than a bathing suit. They soon begin to feel like a second skin and as appropriate for the study of ballet as a bathing suit is for swimming. It is unnecessary to wear pants under the tights, but, if worn, they should be of bikini style and must never show beneath the leotard. The long line of the leg must not be shortened by the outline of an undergarment or by a leotard pulled down to an unflattering straight angle on the thigh. To prevent possible tearing of breast tissue, a well-fitting bra with nonstretching straps should be worn if bra size is 32B or more.

The male dancer wears heavier tights, usually black, and a T-shirt tucked into the tights. Under the tights he wears a dance belt of the same color as the tights, made of elastic and strong cloth, with the wide cloth part worn in front. The dance belt gives more support and protection to the genitals than an ordinary athletic supporter. If a leotard is worn instead of a T-shirt, it is put on after the dance belt but before the tights. To prevent a baggy look, the tights must be pulled up so that they fit firmly at the crotch. They can be secured in this position by elastic suspenders attached to the top of the tights and carried over the shoulders; or a belt can be worn around the waist with the top of the tights rolled over it. (A female dancer sometimes attaches her tights to her bra.)

Ballet Shoes: Ballet dancing usually is associated with "toe-dancing," but beginning students never wear toe shoes (dancers refer to them as point shoes). The hazards of trying to dance in point shoes too soon are discussed on page 137. Beginners, both male and female, wear soft ballet slippers, made of leather or canvas, that have been constructed to give protection while allowing flexibility to the feet. Other soft shoes, such as gymnastic or jazz shoes, do not allow the feet to work properly in ballet exercises, nor do they give the correct "line" to the feet.

The ballet shoe gives the ballet dancer the best possible base from which to work; but it may feel strange indeed when first tried on! The shoe should fit the foot as snugly as a glove fits the hand, but there should still be room for the toes to lie flat, although there must never be extra space at the end of the toes as in a normal street shoe. (Long toenails can result in a misfitted shoe and/or painful bruising later on. See page 139 for proper nail care.) An American-made ballet shoe is purchased usually at least one size, sometimes two sizes, smaller than a street shoe. Individual differences, such as a particularly long big toe, call for different considerations when buying or ordering ballet shoes. It is best to have the teacher check the fit before the student wears the shoes.

The teacher can also show where to sew on the elastic that will keep the heel of the shoe in place. Elastic strips usually come with ballet shoes, but they are seldom sewn on by the manufacturer. Many studios prefer women students to use satin ribbons instead (available at the same shoe store), which are tied around the ankle exactly as ribbons for point shoes. To determine the proper position for the ribbon or elastic on the shoe, fold the heel inward until it lies flat on the sole of the shoe. The elastic or ribbon should be sewn directly in front of this fold.

Like any other shoes, ballet shoes need to be broken in before they are worn for any length of time, such as a period of an entire class. After the teacher has checked the correctness of the fit, the shoes should be softened by bending them back and forth in the hands. Then they can be worn for short periods around the house, but never outside; the soles must be kept free from dirt that might track onto the studio floor. The slight "lump" in the shoe sometimes felt under the ball of the foot will disappear after a few weeks of class. There is no right or left to ballet shoes when they are new. Since the shoes are soft, however, and tend to mold to the feet, most dancers prefer not to switch them once the molding process has begun. The softness of the shoes also causes them to stretch with continual wear, and the resulting looseness can be adjusted by tightening the strings at the front of the shoe. These strings must never hang out but should always be tucked into the shoe.

Getting outfitted for a ballet class involves initial expenses that often are hard on a student budget, but equipment bought for a first class should last for many years if it is properly used and cared for. The shoes, which will be the first item to wear out, should be removed immediately after class and allowed to air before being stored in a dance bag or locker. Since it is unwise and uncomfortable to keep wearing damp practice clothes after class, the student should shower immediately and change into dry clothes. After every class the dance clothes should be washed in mild soap and warm water, with fabric softener added to prolong the stretchiness of the leotards and tights. The garments should be allowed to hang dry as they will shrink in the hot temperatures of most dryers.

Accessories: Students who continue in dance may want to add to their basic dance wardrobe. Dancers are fond of wearing many layers of dance clothing to concentrate heat where it is most needed, removing one or more of these layers as muscles get warm. The most frequent additions to the basic wardrobe are leg warmers, made of a wool or orlon knit and worn over the ordinary dance tights. They typically cover the leg from ankle to hip, although other styles reach to the waist or shoulders. A tight-fitting sweater sometimes is worn, especially in cold weather. The current popularity of dance wear with the general public creates a vast selection of new styles and fabrics to choose from. For class use, however, any dance garment should neither hinder the dancer's movement nor obstruct the clear outline of the body. Teachers frequently refuse to permit students, especially beginners, to wear sweat pants or shirts as a second layer. These bulky garments may feel cozy, but they also may hide serious technical faults or structural problems that can cause weakness or injury. Plastic or rubber suits, although good insulators for keeping muscles warm, seldom are recommended for class attire because they obscure the body outline and, in addition, can lead to dehydration in a warm studio.

Hair should be fastened securely to keep it off the face and neck. The distraction of hair falling into the eyes or whipping about the face in turns or jumps is acute for the student as well as the teacher. Practical aids such as headbands, hair clips or pins, or rubber bands should be used if the hair is long. This applies to men as well as women. When glasses are worn, it is advisable to secure them with a stretch-band, available at sporting goods stores. It is advisable to keep jewelry to a minimum, not only for the important sake of a neat, uncluttered appearance, but also for the sake of safety. Watches, large rings, dangling earrings, and bracelets can be hazardous and distracting to the wearer as well as to other dancers.

ATTENDANCE

Proper equipment and grooming are necessary, but equally important is regular attendance in classes. Attendance should become a habit, for only by regular work will improvement be possible. If one day a student is "not feeling up to par," but is not really ill, perhaps arrangements can be made to observe class. A great deal is learned from watching others.

Taking a technique class in the evening, after a day of hard work, may require great discipline, but, more often than not, the body will respond surprisingly well and be revived by the workout. Exercises and stretches frequently make a person feel better, as is often the case for women with menstrual cramps. The menstrual cycle is a natural female phenomenon, experienced every month for approximately thirty years. Dancers must—and students would do well to—continue their regular activities during menstruation. If a woman has to miss one class a month, she should if possible try to make it up in another section at the same technical level. If many absences occur, the body (and mind) will not be able to catch up with the rest of the class.

BEHAVIOR IN CLASS

More is expected, however, than merely bringing a body to class regularly, for ballet includes the intellectual and emotional being as well as the physical. Studying ballet requires full attention during class; it requires eyes and ears that are open for all available dance clues, a mouth that is closed to chatter and opposed to gumchewing, and a mind and body that are quietly ready for the work ahead.

Alert observation is crucial for learning in a movement discipline such as ballet, where exercises and patterns typically are demonstrated by the instructor for the students to follow. The ability to imitate a movement phrase is important in the highly competitive professional dance world, a world that is virtually closed to those who cannot quickly and correctly reproduce a given movement pattern. For professional and amateur alike, correct performance of a movement helps prevent injury. Although the mind cannot control specific muscles, if it correctly understands the idea of a movement then correct muscles will function when the movement is executed. Correct execution cannot always be achieved simply by unthinkingly copying another's movement pattern. Be open to suggestions; be willing to try new ways of learning; be not afraid to ask questions.

Remember that the face is part of the dance image. Agnes De Mille, choreographer and wise and witty author, has these words of advice for the dance student: "Do not grimace while you practice. Learn to make all the necessary effort with a quiet, controlled face—a quiet face, mark you, not a dull face."[1]

A modicum of good manners is expected in the classroom. For instance, when a progression of movement is to begin from one side of the studio, a slow saunter to the designated area is no more appropriate than a fast sprint to the front of the line. In classes in which there are students of several levels of technique, common protocol is for the more advanced dancers to stand in the front line or to lead off in a combination. In a class of all beginners, it is both wise and courteous to be ready to move to the front but not to expect always to be there. Be aware that everyone in class needs space in which to move. Learning to move while keeping a certain distance from and a certain relationship to other dancers is one of the challenges and rewards of dance study.

If students stop work more than momentarily in a class, they should not start again during that class period. Injuries can occur when cooled muscles are suddenly asked to work vigorously. Similarly, latecomers should not expect to take class if the first exercises have been missed. Dance study is a cumulative experience, each lesson building on the one before, just as the exercises of each lesson build on one another.

Again to quote Miss De Mille: "Do not strain. Use only the muscles needed; relax the others. At the first sign of a cramp in the foot, knee or back, stop and flex the muscles until they ease completely. It is unwise to continue to the point of exhaustion. On the other hand, do not pretend to have pains, or give in easily. . . . Remember always that the point of every exercise is to strengthen and soften, that the object is not how high, how fast, or how long, but how harmonious and how lovely. Do the exercises slowly and carefully at first. Forget speed. Speed will take care of itself later."[2]

THE MUSIC

A piano is commonly found in ballet studios, and the piano accompaniment is a vital part of the classes. At one time the ballet teacher was also the accompanist, playing a small violin as the students performed their exercises and combinations. Today, if a good piano accompanist is not available, a teacher may prefer to use records, perhaps those made especially for ballet classes, with appropriate bands of music for different dance exercises.

Knowledge of music is useful for the study of ballet. Even students who have not studied music will soon learn to count it; that is, they will hear the musical beat or pulse and will recognize a few fundamental musical rhythms and be able to keep time with them.

During ballet classes the instructor probably will demonstrate an exercise and then count it: *1* and 2 and 3 and 4. . . . The numbers are the *beats*, with number 1 having the heaviest beat, or accent. Those four beats make a certain kind of *rhythm* called a 4/4 rhythm (or meter). Series of counts repeated over and over are called *bars* or *measures*. A series of measures is called a *phrase*.

Below are listed the musical rhythms that are used most often in beginning ballet classes. They are divided into measures, as indicated by the / mark. The heavy accent of each rhythm is indicated by underlining the number; the lighter accent, by the symbol ´. Each example is four bars long. Count these rhythms out loud; then try clapping or walking to them, accenting the first count of each measure:

2/4: 1̲ 2/ 1̲ 2/ 1̲ 2/ 1̲ 2/
4/4: 1̲ 2 3́ 4/ 1̲ 2 3́ 4/ 1̲ 2 3́ 4/ 1̲ 2 3́ 4/
3/4: 1̲ 2 3/ 1̲ 2 3/ 1̲ 2 3/ 1̲ 2 3/
6/8: 1̲ 2 3 4́ 5 6/ 1̲ 2 3 4́ 5 6/ 1̲ 2 3 4́ 5 6/ 1̲ 2 3 4́ 5 6/

The speed (*tempo*) of these rhythms can vary from fast (*allegro*) to slow (*adagio*). Dance movements use these same terms: fast steps are called *allegro;* slow, sustained movements are called *adagio* (or the French form, *adage*).

Ballet exercises are usually done an even number of times; that is, a step is repeated four or eight or sixteen times. (Sometimes a step may be done three times with a hold or pause in place of the fourth step.) Similarly, combinations of steps usually are done four or eight times. This is in contrast to modern dance exercises, which often are done an odd number of times (three, five, seven . . .). Moreover, modern dancers frequently use many different rhythms for one dance phrase (such as 1̲ 2 3/ 1̲ 2 3́ 4/ 1̲ 2/ 1̲ 2 3́ 4 . . .). Rarely does a ballet teacher experiment in these ways, although occasionally such experiments may be rewarding.

There are times when a ballet exercise or combination of steps will be learned first in one rhythm, such as 2/4, then tried in another rhythm, such as 6/8. The steps will look and feel slightly different when such a change is made. A change in *tempo* will have an effect also; for example, a faster tempo requires smaller movements covering less space.

To help students know when to be ready to begin an exercise, the accompanist will play a few notes of introduction, which the teacher may count aloud. "Tune in" to these cues and be prepared to move at the designated time, not several beats later.

Beat, rhythm, bar, phrase, tempo—all may seem bewildering to the beginner. A teacher recognizes this and will try to help. For instance, a particular exercise for the leg may be demonstrated and then described by the teacher as "point, lift, point, close." The teacher may then count the exercise as "one, two, three, four." The music will play the same rhythm. Very soon the student will see, hear, and feel that rhythm as 4/4. And in time the student will become equally acquainted with other musical forms, such as the waltz (3/4, with the accent on the first beat), the polka (2/4), and the mazurka (also 3/4, but with the accent on the second beat).

Although responding to the musical beat is fundamental to dance, the classroom would be dull indeed if the musical accompaniment offered merely a flat, steady rhythm. Students' ears should be trained along with their muscles. Phrases of movement and music are the goal—not just steps or notes.

THE VOCABULARY

Because ballet was first nurtured in the royal courts and academies of France, French became the language of the art. All ballet exercises, steps, body positions, and movement directions have French names. These names are in use in every ballet studio the world over, although such wide diffusion has led to certain differences, even corruption in specific terminology.

It is advantageous to have studied French, but students who have not will soon have a number of French words in their vocabulary after a few classes in ballet. These words are quite specific, and their use can greatly simplify directions that a teacher might otherwise have to use. In addition, the terminology simplifies the task of writing down class work or choreography, should that sometime be necessary or desirable.

The technical vocabulary used in this book is based primarily on that used by the National Academy of Ballet. Under the direction of Thalia Mara, this academy tried to standardize ballet terminology according to its most common usage today.

STYLE

As might be expected, such a global art includes some regional differences in training and in the manner in which steps and poses are executed—differences in style. Briefly described, the French have emphasized charm and elegance, whereas the Italian school has stressed technical virtuosity. The Russian school was founded by French ballet masters, but later it adopted and adapted the more brilliant technique of the Italians. The combination of these and other sources produced the strength and flair characteristic of Russian dancers. In contrast, the British style is less flamboyant, more serene. The Danish school has maintained the exuberant lightness and speed of its nineteenth-century mentor, Auguste Bournonville. The methods of two outstanding teachers, Enrico Cecchetti (1850–1928) and Agrippina Vaganova (1879–1951), have created methods of technique now being handed down by their many pupils. There is emerging an American style, a blend of French, Italian, and Russian influences with a distinctive dose of American restless energy and youthful spirit.

The style of a class will reflect one of these or other schools, depending on the training of the teacher. It is unwise, therefore, for the beginning student to study with more than one teacher, unless the teachers share a common technical background and philosophy of teaching. American dancers are beset with an urgent quest toward greater and greater technical achievements that frequently propels them to one instructor or school after another. The result of such frantic effort can be confusion in technique and ambiguity in style.

This book is offered as a general ballet text, rather than a presentation of one particular instructional method. It does, however, reflect much of the author's training with Margaret Craske in the Cecchetti Method and with Thalia Mara and Arthur Mahoney of the National Academy of Ballet.

A first class in ballet may seem more like a lesson in basic anatomy than a dancing class. Without an understanding of proper body alignment and placement, there can be no progress in work toward balance, form, and freedom and economy of movement. In addition, the very exercises that lead to control, strength, and beauty of line in ballet can also lead to weaknesses and injuries when attempted by a poorly aligned body.

ALIGNMENT

Alignment in ballet essentially means good posture; that is, the various body parts—head, shoulders, arms, ribs, hips, legs, feet—are in correct relative position with one another. Bad posture can result in a slump, with rounded shoulders and droopy head, or a sway, with the pelvis released backward, causing a hollow look to the lower back. These distortions in alignment are detrimental enough to an ordinary body, but they can be positively hazardous for the ballet student. "Any departure from the balanced posture will strain muscles and ligaments and cause undue friction in joints—if one segment of the body is out of line, all others will be affected."[3]

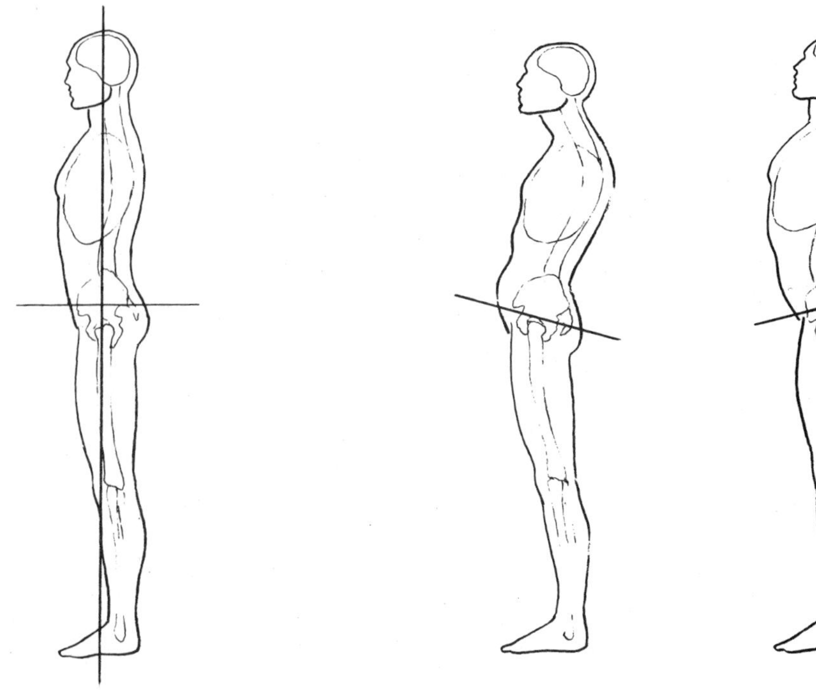

Good posture

Poor posture

Ballet placement refers to a well-aligned body that is shifted slightly forward from the ankle over the ball of the foot. A dancer is said to be "placed" when the muscles of the body have become educated to assume a position of correct alignment without effort. Once achieved, good posture requires less effort to maintain than poor posture. Correct placement is a slow process, however, requiring many classes, often many years of work. In ballet the body is always active, not static, thus requiring a dynamic, yet subtle "realigning" as it assumes new and different poses.

Few dancers or ballet teachers use specific anatomical terminology, yet their language can convey the fundamentals of correct alignment necessary for ballet. It is helpful to contemplate these fundamentals one at a time, keeping in mind that the goal is to find the most efficient posture for the work ahead.

The Feet: To begin an understanding of proper alignment and placement for ballet, stand with the feet a few inches apart, pointing straight ahead (sometimes called *parallel* position). The feet should feel relaxed, the toes flat, with the weight of the body resting mainly on three points: the heel, the base of the big toe, and the little toe. In this position, as in the ballet positions discussed later, the arch of the foot is supported, the ankles are prevented from rolling inward or outward, and the body is given a strong base from which to work.

The Legs: Straighten the knees firmly, *but do not push them back*. They should be directly over the feet. Now bend the knees, keeping the heels on the floor, and check to see that the knees are pointing directly over the front of the feet. This knee-over-foot alignment is correct for any bend of the knees, whether in this parallel position or in the turned-out positions of ballet. Begin to straighten the knees, and also begin to sense a lengthening of the thighs.

The Torso: The pelvis should be in a midway position, neither tucking under nor sticking out. To check this position, place the palm of one hand on the abdomen (which ought to feel flat and pulled up) and the back of the other hand on the lower spine (the "small of the back"). The front hand should be perpendicular to the floor and the back hand nearly so. The natural curves of the spine, which allow it to be flexible and to absorb shock, must be neither exaggerated nor entirely flattened out. Maintaining a firm abdomen and an extended spine will help achieve correct alignment in a more efficient way than the oft-misunderstood admonition to "tuck under your hips."

The rib cage should be directly in line with the hips. Any lift of the ribs should coincide with the lengthening, not shortening, of the spine. At no time should the rib cage feel rigid or forced forward; breathing should remain normal.

To feel the correct position of shoulders, lift them up toward the ears, hold them there a few seconds, and then let them drop. Now feel the shoulder blades resting downward. The shoulders will be low but not pulled backward. Let the arms hang naturally from this position.

The Head: The head must be in alignment with the ribs and hips. The back of the neck is kept long, for it is a continuation of the spine, on which the head lightly rests. The chin is parallel to the floor, but never thrust forward. The eyes look forward, not down.

Other Methods: In the 1980s it is not unusual to find lessons in body alignment occurring with students not standing, as described above, but lying on the floor. New approaches to movement, changes in habitual muscle patterns, release of tensions, as well as more efficient posture are some of the goals of well-known body therapy methods developed by such pioneers as Lulu Sweigard, Irmgard Bartenieff, and Moshe Feldenkrais. Such body therapy methods are being integrated into the work of some dancers and instructors as they seek new and more appropriate ways of performing, teaching, and, not least, aligning the bones of the body.

TURNOUT

The student must also deal with another essential element related to alignment: the turnout of the legs at the hip joints. The legs are rotated outward from that joint *only as far as that position can be maintained without disturbing the body alignment.* Ideally, this turnout is 180 degrees, but it is very seldom realistic for most beginning students (children or adults). Individual differences in body structure and strength should determine the degree of turnout. Whatever that degree, the arches of the feet must remain lifted and the ankles straight. Remember that the weight of the body rests on the base of the big and little toes and the heel. For correct ballet placement, this weight should be shifted slightly forward from the ankle so that it rests more on the balls of the feet than back on the heels. In maintaining this position it is important that the pelvis not release backward or push forward. The knees should always be in line with the feet, following the same rule of alignment as in the parallel position: When the knees are bent, they ought to be over the center of the feet.

Realistic turnout for many beginners

Although this position may feel strange at first, it is important to understand that the turnout of the legs in ballet is merely an exaggeration of a perfectly normal action for the human body. The top of the thigh bone can rotate either inward or outward in the hip socket. Ballet technique simply has capitalized on the outward rotation possibility. In maintaining the turnout, there should be no sense of strain or tension. The body must not be stiff and locked in position. It must be firm, yet at ease and free to move.

THE FIVE POSITIONS OF THE FEET

The five positions of the feet are the foundations of ballet technique. Every step, every movement, every pose relates in some way to one or more of these positions. In all five positions the weight must be equally distributed on both feet, the legs straight unless purposefully flexed (bent). The ideal positions are illustrated and described on the following page.

First position: the legs turned out from the hips, the heels and knees touching, the feet forming a straight line

Second position: the legs turned out from the hips, as in first position, but the heels about twelve inches apart

Third position: the legs turned out from the hips, one foot directly in front of the other, with the heel of each foot touching the middle of the other foot

Fourth position: the legs turned out from the hips, one foot either directly in front of the other and one short step apart (for crossed fourth position) or forward from first position (for open fourth position)

Fifth position: the legs turned out from the hips, one foot directly in front of the other, with the heel of the front foot at the joint of the toe of the back foot

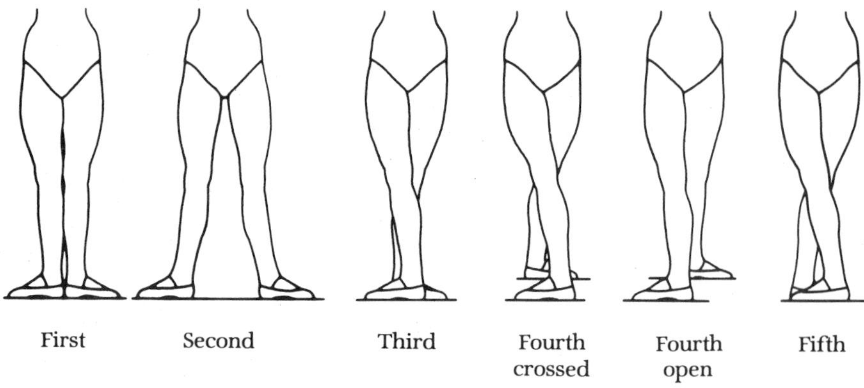

Historically, complete turnout developed slowly—by 1700 the angle of turnout was 90 degrees; by 1800 it was 180 degrees. A similar progression is mirrored in a student's training; a beginner works from positions of lesser turnout, advancing gradually as the body learns to maintain correct alignment in the more extreme positions. This must be a slow and careful process.

At the beginning of training it is wise to begin and end exercises in first position; later exercises can be done from third, and finally from the more demanding fifth position.

SPECIAL CONSIDERATIONS

A dancer's body is expected to be centered, the weight of the body resting evenly on both feet while imaginary lines dissect the body vertically from head to toe and horizontally across the body at hip level. A shift of weight to one foot, with the other leg extended or raised, brings a challenge to this sense of center. To be properly balanced on one leg, the dancer must maintain the vertical line as the weight is shifted. That line must not tip to one side or too far forward or backward. The horizontal line must be maintained across the hips. The temptations to "sit" into the supporting leg or to raise the other hip along with the leg must be discouraged. These principles need to be understood and mastered in basic exercises before the beginner attempts more complicated movements or positions that would otherwise distort the center of balance.

Properly balanced   Improperly balanced

All five positions of the feet can be done with the heels raised and the weight on the balls of the feet. In beginning work these are done to quarter point and half point; after sufficient strength is acquired they can be done to three-quarter point. Many steps and poses are taken in these raised positions.

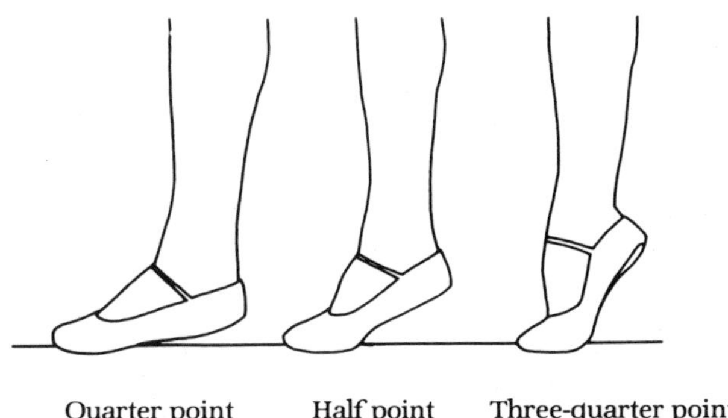

Quarter point   Half point   Three-quarter point

Practice
Stand with the feet parallel. Lift one heel as high as possible while keeping the ball of that foot firmly on the floor. The ankle and knee should be in line with the big toe and the second toe. Now try practicing this position with the legs turned out. If the foot leans toward only the big toe or toward the little toe, it

is said to be "sickled," a potentially harmful position for the ankles and knees, as well as the feet.

When pointing the foot, it is wise to remember that it is the entire foot that moves and not just the toes.

Practice

Sit on the floor, or well back in a chair, legs together and straight, the feet flexed (bent) at the ankles. Slowly begin arching the feet, working inch by inch from the ankle through the insteps of the feet to the balls of the feet, and then to the toes. The knees should remain straight. The toes should appear as a continuation of the arch of the pointed foot, creating a smooth line with the leg. The toes are pressed together but not "knuckled under."

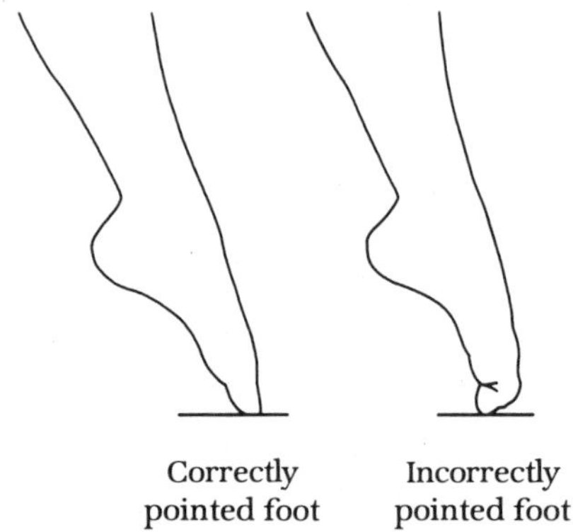

Correctly pointed foot — Incorrectly pointed foot

WARM-UP

Dancers frequently like to limber their bodies gently before the actual class begins. This warm-up can help awaken the muscles, as well as the mind, for the work ahead. Some teachers may even begin the lesson with such preparatory exercises, not leaving it to beginners to warm up on their own. Following are examples of simple movements that may be used as a warm-up. Note that these are done slowly and without jumps or extreme stretches:

Practice

To warm the neck area: Bend the head forward, then lift the face toward the ceiling; tilt the head from side to side; turn the head from side to side; roll the head in a circle.

To warm the chest area: Lift the shoulders toward the ears, let them drop; circle the shoulders; circle the arms forward, up, and back.

To stretch out the entire body: Reach upward, sideward, and forward.

To activate the reflexes: Bend slowly forward, starting with the head and "rolling" down through each vertebra of the spine. "Hang" in this forward position with the body relaxed, the knees either straight or slightly bent. Reverse the movements, returning to an upright position with the body in correct alignment. Do this in parallel position, then in first position.

To warm the ankles and feet: Circle the foot at the ankle; flex and point the foot (as described above); lift the heel of one foot while pressing the ball of that foot on the floor; complete the arching of the foot by pointing through the toes and allowing them to leave the floor slightly. Reverse the action by rolling down through the toes to the ball of the foot, then lowering the heel.

To warm up the hip joint: Lift the knee several times to the front; gently swing the leg forward and backward.

CORRECT BREATHING

Ballet students must breathe correctly in order to sustain the vigor necessary for a strenuous class. This means deep or diaphragmatic breathing, in which air is inhaled through the nose (not the mouth) and the middle and lower lungs filled with air. Shallow breathing (where only the upper, smaller part of the lung is used) does not give the dancer enough oxygen. Yawns during a class can indicate lack of oxygen rather than lack of interest.

Breathing during exercises will not be in a constant, even rhythm, however. The body will naturally want to inhale longer or more quickly, depending upon the difficulty of an exercise. The dancer learns to inhale more deeply before movements requiring greater effort, and to hold the breath in order to sustain a leap or a balance.

Raoul Gelabert, dance therapist, suggests the following exercise to develop deeper breathing:

> Stand, arms at the side, and breathe in through the nose, filling the abdomen with one deep breath. Holding the breath, bend forward, allowing the spine to curve, sharply contract and exhale the air through the mouth. With the abdomen completely empty of air, return to the upright position. Repeat.[4]

The releasing of muscular tension by this exercise also contributes to a gentle stretch, sensed especially in the lower back and down the legs.

NOTES

1. Agnes de Mille, *To a Young Dancer* (Boston: Little, Brown, 1960), 24.
2. *Ibid.*
3. Donald F. Featherstone, *Dancing Without Danger* (South Brunswick and New York: Barnes, 1970), 65.
4. Raoul Gelabert, *Anatomy for the Dancer*, vol. 2 (New York: Dance Magazine, 1966), 55.

CHAPTER 3
BALLET TECHNIQUE: *BARRE* WORK

The first formal segment of classroom instruction begins with exercises done at the *barre*. Although each exercise has its own purpose, *barre* work as a whole is designed to strengthen the feet, legs, and back; to increase range of movement (especially at the hip); to attain balance and control; to stabilize turnout; and to gain speed in the feet and lightness in the legs—in other words, to instill the "mechanics" of ballet technique.

USE OF THE *BARRE*

The *barre* itself is meant as a hand support only, steadying the body but not bearing its weight. In the early stages of training, while doing many exercises the student faces the *barre* with both hands resting lightly on it, close together, and the elbows relaxed and slightly bent. This position gives the beginner an extra aid in centering the body, because the hips and shoulders can be kept parallel with the horizontal line of the *barre*. Later, most exercises are done with the body sideways to the *barre*, one hand on the *barre* somewhat forward of the shoulder, the fingers resting on top of the *barre* with the thumb along the side of the *barre* rather than below it. The body should be far enough from the *barre* to allow the elbow to be relaxed and slightly bent.

Before an exercise begins, the free arm "prepares" by rising forward to the level of the fork in the ribs and then opening out to the side, where it usually remains throughout the exercise. The leg farther from the *barre* (the "outside" leg) does the exercise. Since exercises traditionally begin with the right leg, the dancer begins with the left hand on the *barre*. To help avoid a certain "right-leggedness" in dancers, it is wise to begin exercises occasionally on the other side. Sometimes, too, it is helpful to "prepare" with both arms, raising them forward so that the hands are centered on the torso, opening them outward to the side, and then taking the *barre* with the inside hand. When an exercise is completed, both arms are lowered, and the final position is held momentarily before turning to repeat the exercise with the other leg.

The amount of class time spent in *barre* work diminishes as technical ability improves. The variety of exercises—and also the number of times an exercise is done—actually increases with advancing levels of technique, but movements are done more quickly and therefore take less time. Beginners may spend most of their early classes at the *barre*, with the time being gradually reduced to about one-half of the period, but never to less than one-third. The length of an entire class is commonly one and a half hours, although scheduling patterns in colleges and universities often necessitate shorter sessions.

SEQUENCE OF EXERCISES

No universally accepted order of sequence for *barre* exercises exists, except that most classes begin with the most basic movement of ballet, the *plié*, or bend of the knees, and finish with the vigorous movements of the *grand battement*, or large beating action of the leg. Although the sequence varies somewhat from teacher to teacher and from school to school, in general the smaller, slower movements are done first, legs are gradually warmed up from the feet to the knees to the hips, and combinations of movements grow from simple to more complex. The *barre* exercises discussed in the following pages are arranged in broad general categories that do not reflect any preferred order of teaching. Because they lay the foundation for the entire technique of ballet, they will be described in some detail, the three most fundamental exercises deserving first attention. But it must be remembered that the most specific instructions, cautions, or hints from a printed page cannot *teach* the mechanics of ballet even to the most willing student. Neither can the finest illustrations. Therefore, this is not intended as a how-to-do-it section, but rather as a resource for, and supplement to, classroom study.

THREE FUNDAMENTAL EXERCISES: *PLIÉ, RELEVÉ, BATTEMENT TENDU*

The following three exercises represent ballet's most fundamental movements of the legs—bending and straightening the knees, raising and lowering the heels, and stretching the foot along the floor before returning it to a closed position.

PLIÉ (plee-AY)

Definition: A *plié* is a bending movement of the knees. A half-bend is called a *demi-plié;* a deep bend, a *grand plié.* (Technically, a bend on only one leg is not a *plié*, but a *fondu*.)

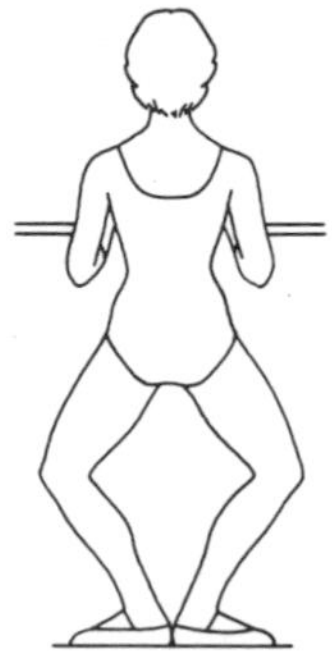

Demi-plié
in first position

Purpose: Almost every step in ballet—certainly every jumping movement—involves a bending movement of the legs. The correct execution of the *demi-plié* (and the *fondu*) gives a springy quality to steps of elevation and a lightness to all dance movements. The *grand plié* is important in stretching and strengthening the legs, since the entire weight of the upper body is lowered and raised by the legs. Both *demi-plié* and *grand plié* require even distribution of the weight on both feet, thus making it easier to center the body and to master the turnout of the legs. Both types of *plié* increase the circulation of the blood in the legs, thus facilitating warm-up. Knowing how and when to bend the knees is the cornerstone of ballet technique.

Description: *Pliés* are done in all positions of the feet. During the *demi-plié* the heels never leave the floor. The movement begins in the high, inner side of the thighs; the knees open in a direct line over the toes until the depth of the *demi-plié* is reached (determined by the length of the Achilles tendon connecting the calf muscle and the heel); then the legs return to their original straight position.

Grand plié in first position

The *grand plié* begins exactly as the *demi-plié,* but when the maximum stretch of the Achilles tendon is felt, the heels are allowed to release from the floor, and the knees continue to bend over the feet until, ideally, the thighs are almost parallel with the floor. Immediately the action is reversed: The heels press into the floor, the knees straighten, and the thighs continue to pull up until the original position is attained. The *grand plié* thus described is done in all positions except the second and the open fourth positions, where, because of the spread of the legs, the heels need not and should not be released from the floor.

Demi-plié and *grand plié* in second position

Caution: In all *pliés* the body must be centered over the feet, the spine must remain straight, with the pelvis in the midway position—that is, neither pushed forward nor released backward. The feet must be securely placed on the floor but not tense, with the arches supported so they do not roll. The weight of the body must not settle into the knees at the depth of the *grand plié*. The movement of the *plié* should be smooth and slow but without pauses at any point in the exercise. The straightening of the legs must be done as carefully as the bending of them. When the legs are crossed, as in third, fourth, and fifth positions, it is important that the weight continue to be distributed evenly on both feet (the temptation often is to lean toward the back foot). These crossed positions also require great care in opening the knees equally, so that one knee lowers to the same level as the other (the tendency often is to drop the back knee, especially in

Incorrect *pliés*

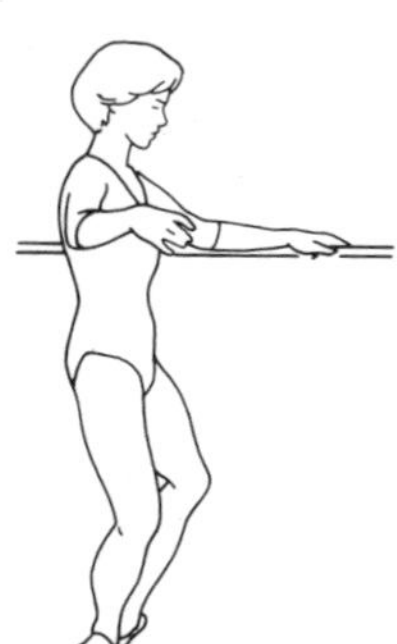

Arches rolling and knees forward

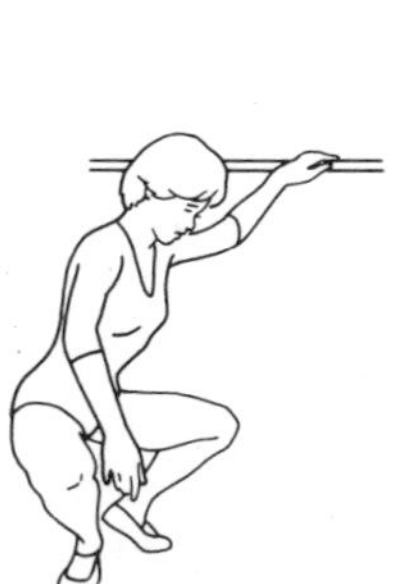

Weight settled into knees

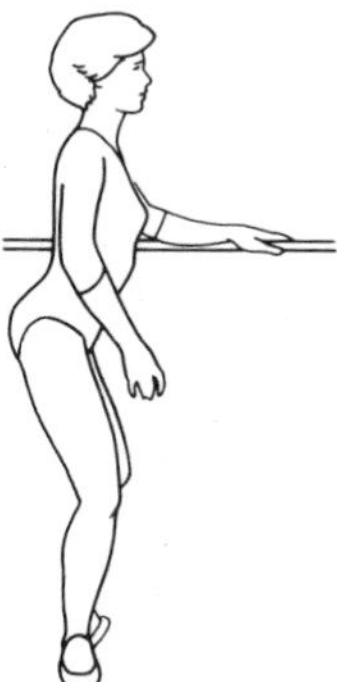

Pelvis released backward

the fourth position). The depth of the *grand plié* is determined by the strength of the muscles on the inner side of the thighs and by the length of the Achilles tendon. Therefore, the thighs ought not to be lowered all the way to the horizontal position unless correct body alignment can be maintained throughout the *plié*.

Suggestions: Learn to execute the *demi-plié* correctly before attempting the *grand plié*. Begin the study of *pliés* in the first and second positions; later add the third position and when sufficient strength has developed, the fourth and fifth positions (when changing to a new position, move only one foot and do not look at it). Learn the *pliés* facing the *barre* before trying them sideways or with movements of the arm.

Because *grands pliés* are an especially strenuous exercise for the knees, they should be limited in number and performed after the legs are warmed up. Thus, while *demi-pliés* are appropriate as a first exercise, *grands pliés* may be more safely and effectively performed later in the *barre* sequence.

RELEVÉ (ruh-leh-VAY)

Definition: A *relevé* is a rise to the ball of the foot, or, as often termed, to the *demi-pointe*. The rise is sometimes called *elevé* when it is made without the benefit of a preceding *plié*. Literally, *relevé* means "relifted."

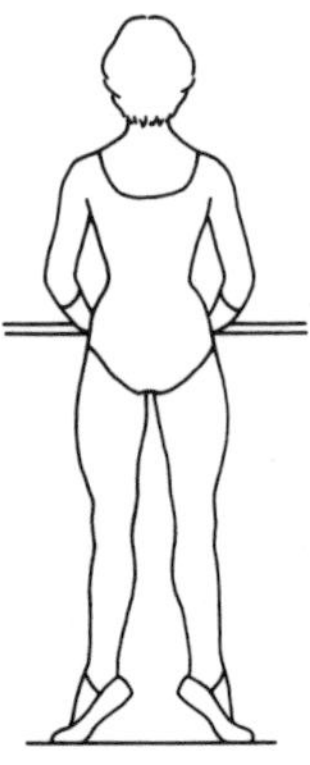

Relevé to three-quarter point

Purpose: Strength, suppleness, and control of the feet are developed by this exercise. When the thighs pull up in the *relevé*, the knees and the muscles of the legs are strengthened also. The *relevé* builds a strong, secure *demi-pointe* position, which is so important for balance, turns, and many steps of ballet. It is a necessary preparation for work that later may be done on a full point by advanced students (traditionally, women only). As an exercise in combination with *pliés*, the *relevé* serves also as a preparation for jumps.

Description: *Relevés* are done in all positions of the feet. For the simplest (*elevé*), the heels are lifted (the weight of the body going to the *demi-pointes*) and then lowered back to their original position without a bend of the knees. There are three levels of *demi-pointe*—quarter, half, and three-quarter—which denote the relative distance of the heels from the floor. The *relevé* may go to any one of these levels, but ultimately the greatest benefit is derived when the student moves slowly through all the levels to the highest, and then returns just as slowly until the heels touch the floor.

A *relevé* preceded and followed by a *demi-plié* requires a high degree of coordination; the lift of the heels must be timed with the straightening of the knees, and the lowering of the heels with the bending of the knees. The action can be smooth with the heels raised and lowered in the same spot, or it can be quick and springy with a firm push against the floor from the *demi-plié* to the *relevé* position.

Two basic springing *relevés* are the *soussus* and the *échappé*. The *soussus* (soo-siu) is a *relevé* made with a slight spring from fifth position *demi-plié* to a tight fifth position on *demi-pointes*, the feet moving equally toward the center of the body. The *échappé* (ay-shah-PAY) is a *relevé* made with a slight spring from fifth position *demi-plié* to an open position on *demi-pointes* (to second position; later to fourth), the feet moving equally from the center of the body. After both types of springing *relevés*, the feet return to their original position in *demi-plié*, also by means of a slight spring.

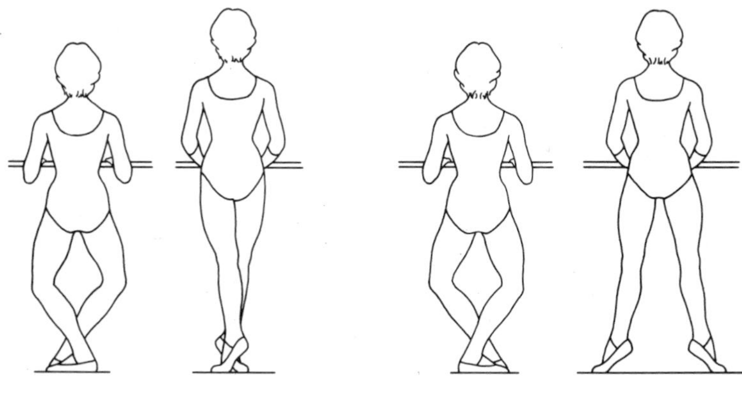

Soussus *Échappé relevé*

Relevés also can be taken to only one foot following a *demi-plié* from any of the five positions of the feet or from a position in *fondu.* The raised foot, well pointed and turned out, usually is brought in front or in back of the supporting ankle or knee. From there it can return to a *demi-plié* position, or it can remain lifted while the supporting foot lowers into a *fondu* position.

Cautions: In all *relevés* on two feet, the body must be centered over both feet. The turnout of the legs must be maintained throughout the raising and lowering of the heels. In the *demi-pointe* position: (1) The weight of the body should be pulled up as much as possible so that it rests lightly on the ball of the foot, toward the first three toes (beginners should never *relevé* to the full point; this is done only by advanced women students who wear shoes specially constructed for work on full point). (2) The feet must never be allowed to roll either in or out because that weakens the ankles and the arches of the feet. (3) The knees must be straight.

Suggestions: Learn the *elevé* in first and second positions; later practice it in the other positions of the feet. When the principles of *elevé* have been mastered, add the *relevés* from *demi-plié*, beginning with those requiring slow, smooth action. Later try the springing *relevés*, and later still the *relevés* to one foot. All *relevés* first should be practiced facing the *barre.*

BATTEMENT TENDU (baht-MAH*n* tah*n*-DIU)

Definition: Literally, *battement* means "beating." In ballet the term refers to almost every leg movement at the *barre.* There are over twenty types of *battements,* but the most fundamental is the *battement tendu,* often simply called tendu ("stretched"). In this exercise, the working foot, starting from a closed position, is stretched along the floor and returned to its original position at the supporting leg.

Purpose: More than any exercise, the *battement tendu* strengthens the foot by alternating tension and relaxation as it is moved along the floor. The *tendu* is basic to many other exercises and steps of ballet, and, as typically the first exercise done with one leg at the *barre,* it is basic to the centering of the body on the supporting leg.

Description: In *battements tendus* the toes never leave the floor. The whole foot slides out from the closed position (first, third, or fifth) until the heel has to be raised in order not to shift the weight off the supporting leg. Immediately the foot begins to arch, first through the instep and then through the ball of the foot until the maximum stretch of the *tendu* is reached. To return to the starting position, first the ball of the foot relaxes and then the instep, until all tension is released and the heel is placed firmly on the floor. Both legs may remain straight throughout the exercise, or they may finish in a *demi-plié* in the closed position. *Tendus* are done to the front, to the side, and to the back. When an exercise is done consecutively to these directions, it is said to be done *en croix* (ahn krwah)—in the shape of a cross.

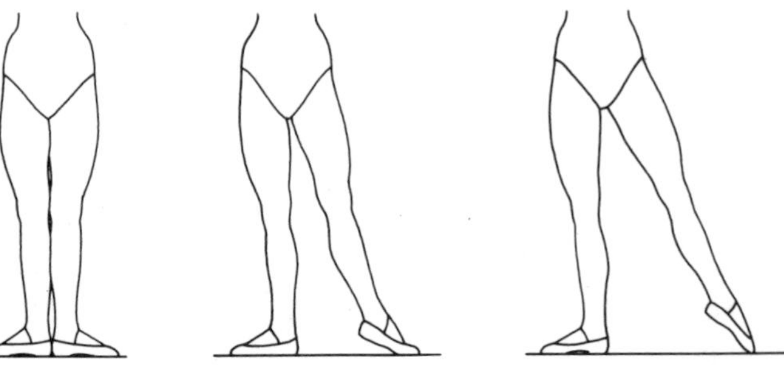

Battement tendu à la seconde

When the tips of the toes touch the floor, foot fully arched and knee straight, the position is termed *pointe tendue* (pwah*n*t tah*n*-DIU)—"point stretched."

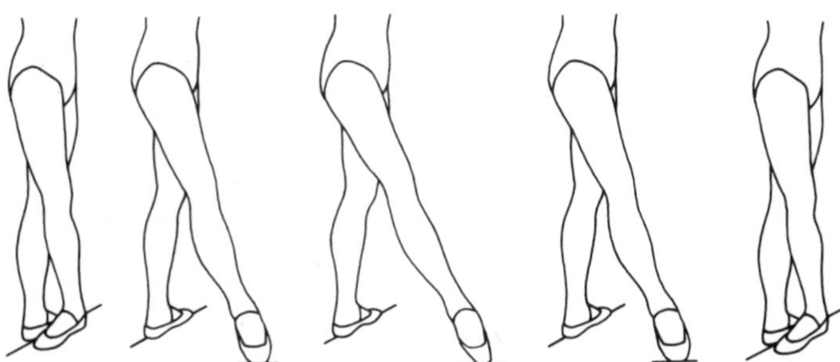

Battement tendu à la quatrième devant

Cautions: Correct body alignment must be maintained at all times, special care being taken not to "sit" into the supporting hip or to allow the lower back to shorten. The supporting foot must not roll, nor must any weight shift to the extended foot, thus putting pressure on the pointed toes. The knee of the working leg must not bend as the leg opens or closes. Proper turnout can be maintained throughout the exercise by attending to the suggestions offered below.

Suggestions: In *battements tendus* to the side, the movement of the foot should travel along a path indicated by the degree of turnout, in other words, in the direction of the toes. Properly speaking, this direction is *à la seconde,* rather than "to the side."

In *battements tendus* to the front (*à la quatrième devant*), the heel leads the way forward so that the bone at the inside of the ankle remains forward as much as possible. As the foot returns, the toes lead the way to the closed position, and the inside ankle bone remains forward. In this way correct alignment is maintained and the foot does not "sickle."

Correct alignment

Incorrect alignment

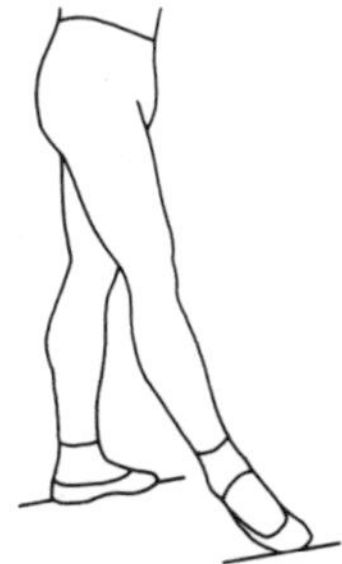

Incorrect or "sickled" position

The process is reversed for *battements tendus* to the back (*à la quatrième derrière*): The toes lead the way backward, the heel leads the way for the return, with the bone at the outside of the ankle pointing backward as much as possible throughout the exercise. Take care not to drop the head forward or to shorten the lower back by releasing the pelvis from its upright position. In *battements tendus* to the front or side, the foot should point to the tip of the big toe (and often of the second toe as well). However, when performed to the back, the point is to the tip of the *side* of the big toe.

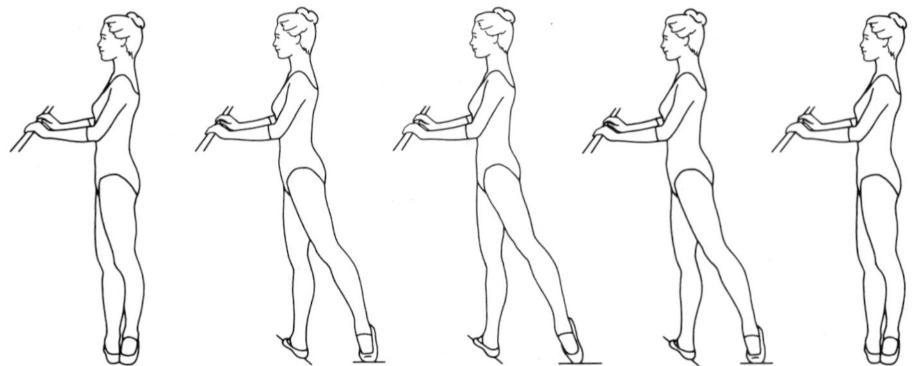

Battement tendu à la quatrième derrière

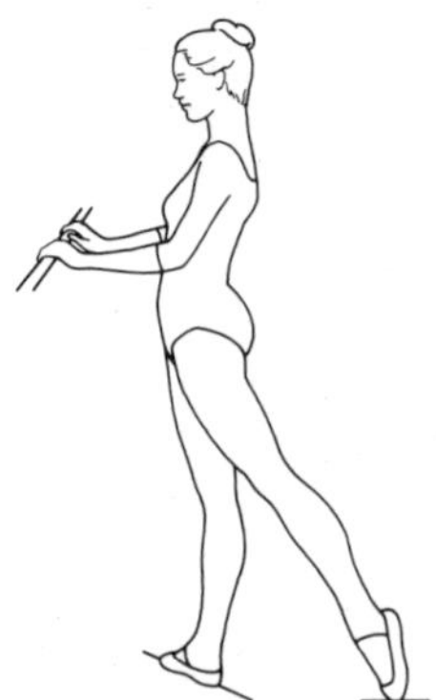

Incorrect *battement* alignment

Begin the study of this exercise by stretching the foot *à la seconde* from first position, later from third position (better to use a good third than a poor fifth position), closing in front each time for a series of *battements*, then closing in back each time. Later the closings can alternate front and back of the supporting foot.

Battements tendus forward or backward are best learned from third position (and later practiced from fifth position) rather than first position because the point of the foot in line with the crossed position gives a clearer concept of the basic front direction (*quatrième devant*) and back direction (*quatrième derrière*).

In a beginning class, a series of *battements* are best done only in one direction before changing to another direction. They should first be practiced slowly and evenly. Gradually speed can be increased and an accent given to the closing of each *battement.*

OTHER BASIC *BATTEMENTS*

The following *battement* exercises represent beating actions of the leg when it is either extended or bent. These four fundamental movements can be thought of as disengaged, stretched-and-lifted, struck, and out-and-in actions.

BATTEMENT DÉGAGÉ (baht-MAH*n* day-gah-ZHAY)

Definition: A *dégagé* is a *battement* disengaged from the floor; it is sometimes called *battement tendu jeté* ("thrown"), *battement glissé* ("glided"), or simply *dégagé* ("disengaged").

Purpose: The chief function of the *dégagé* is to develop speed in pointing the feet. It helps the arches and ankles to become supple and prepares them for the quick movements in jumps. The rapid opening and closing of the leg is the foundation for *allegro* steps with beats (*batterie*). The *dégagé* itself is part of many ballet steps, such as *sissonne.*

Description: The movement begins in the same way as *battement tendu,* but the action continues so that the working foot leaves the floor a few inches, well pointed, before sliding back to the closed position. The action can be described as a brush of the foot.

Cautions: The advice for the correct execution of *battements tendus* is equally applicable for *battements dégagés,* except that the toes are allowed to leave the floor. Care must be taken, however, that the toes rise only a very few inches. If the leg is raised too high, the capacity for speed is lost. Faults in many *allegro* steps can be traced to errors made in *dégagés,* especially the failure to touch the pointed toes on the floor before sliding the foot to the closed position. The timing of the exercise should emphasize the closing of the *dégagé.*

Suggestions: As in *battements tendus,* the study of *dégagés* begins in first position with the movement done *à la seconde.* It can be broken down as follows: Brush away from the closed position (finishing with the foot slightly off the floor); touch the toes to the floor; slide the foot back to the closed position. Each part of the exercise can receive a separate count with another count for a hold in the closed position (to allow time for the foot to relax): Brush (count 1), touch the toes (count 2), close (count 3), hold the position (count 4). Later, it can be done in two counts: Brush (count 1), touch the toes (and), close (count 2), hold (and). Eventually the *dégagé* is done with the entire movement happening on the "and," with the closing to position on the count. The breakdown of the exercise can, of course, also be followed in learning *dégagés* to the front and to the back, and from third or fifth position.

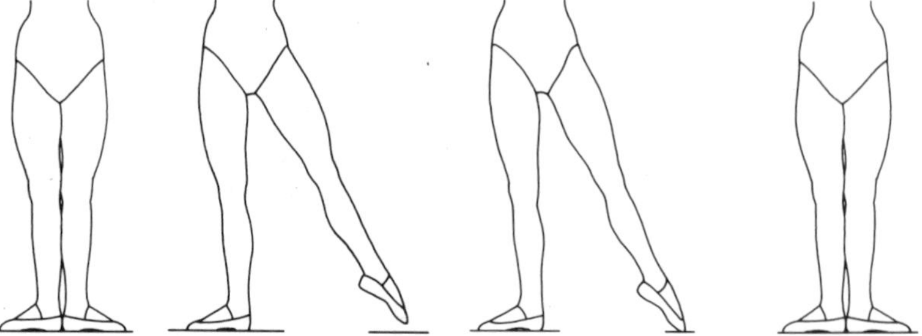

Battement dégagé à la seconde

GRAND BATTEMENT (grahn baht-MAH*n*)

Definition: The *grand battement* is a large beating action of the leg, another continuation of the basic *battement tendu.*

Purpose: The forceful "throw" of the leg into the air limbers and stretches the legs (especially at the backs of the thighs). It helps to loosen the hip joint, while at the same time strengthening the control of the hip muscles. Properly done, the *grand battement* creates a lightness in the legs necessary for steps of high elevation such as *grand jeté.* It also increases the height of the extension of the legs, valuable for *développés* and other exercises of *adagio.*

Description: The movement begins in the same way as the *tendu* but is continued upward to hip height (higher or lower, depending on the stretch and control of the body); then the leg is lowered with control until the toes touch the floor and the foot closes as in *battement tendu. Grands battements* are done to the front, to the side, and to the back.

Cautions: Follow all the basic rules of the *battement tendu*, being especially careful not to raise the hip of the working leg or allow the thighs to turn in. The movement is done by the working leg only. To achieve the desired lightness of the leg, its lift should be initiated by the brush of the foot along the floor, not by the "pickup" of the thigh. The knees must not bend, nor should the heel of the supporting foot leave the floor. The torso remains stationary except during the *grand battement* to the back. In that exercise the weight is allowed to shift *slightly* forward, permitting the leg to lift more freely to the back and relieving possible tensions in the spine and shoulders. The shift must be very slight; the body must not rock back and forth or twist toward the lifted leg. After the lift of the leg to the back, the body must return to its upright position as the foot closes.

Height of the leg for *grand battement à la quatrième devant, à la seconde, à la quatrième derrière* at 90 degrees

Suggestions: Practice *grands battements* at forty-five degrees until proper placement and turnout can be maintained at ninety degrees or higher. Break down the exercise as follows: From a closed position (first, third, or fifth), slide the foot to *pointe tendue* (count 1), lift the leg (count 2), lower the leg to *pointe tendue* (count 3), and slide the foot to the closed position (count 4). Later try the exercise in three counts instead of four: Brush the leg into the air (count 1), lower it to *pointe tendue* (count 2), and return it to the closed position (count 3). Eventually the exercise is to be done with the entire movement happening on "and," with the closing of the foot on the count.

Incorrect *battements*

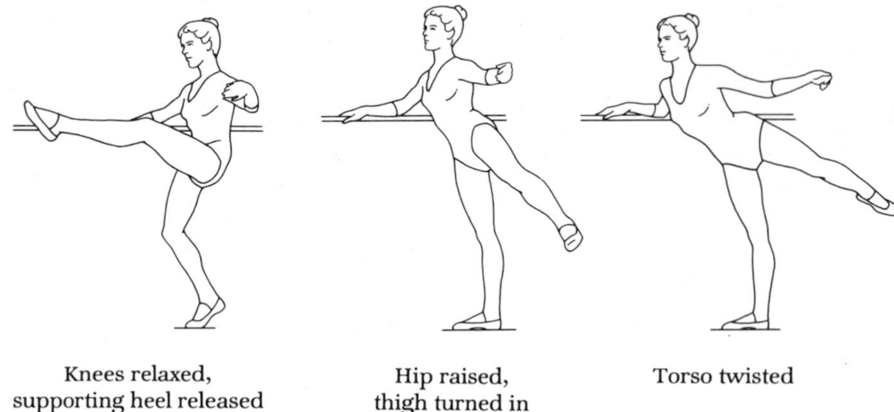

Knees relaxed, supporting heel released

Hip raised, thigh turned in

Torso twisted

BATTEMENT FRAPPÉ (baht-MAH*n* frah-PAY)

Definition: A *battement frappé* is a strong brush of the ball of the foot from a position at the ankle of the supporting leg; it is often called simply *frappé*, which means "struck."

Purpose: The constant releasing and pointing of the foot in *battements frappés* greatly strengthen the ankles and feet. The muscles in the sole of the foot are stimulated and strengthened by the brush of the ball of the foot against the floor in the outward movement. Done quickly, the *frappé* builds speed and flexibility in the feet, directly related to many jumps in ballet, particularly the *jeté*.

Description: The *battement frappé à la seconde* begins with the working foot slightly flexed and the heel touching just above the front of the ankle of the supporting foot. The ball of the working foot then brushes strongly against the floor to *dégagé* position *à la seconde*. It then returns to the back of the ankle without touching the floor, ready to begin again. An alternate starting position for the working foot is *pointe tendue à la seconde*. It is then brought to the supporting ankle, where the exercise continues as described.

Cautions: Do not "sit" into the supporting leg or allow the toes of the working foot to release upwards. The thigh of the working leg must not lift; the action of the *frappé* happens from the knee down. The ball of the foot, not just the tips of the toes, should brush briskly along the floor but should never pound against the surface. Both the knee and foot of the working leg should be taut at the finish of the brush.

Suggestions: In the early stages, the *frappé* can be done in four counts: Brush to the extended position just off the floor (count 1), hold this position (count 2), return to the position at the supporting leg (count 3), hold (count 4).

Later a 3/4 rhythm can be tried: Brush and hold the position (counts 1, 2), return to the supporting leg (count 3). Eventually the *frappé* is done on one count, with the accent on the brush outward and the return on the "and." The exercise can later be done to the front and to the back as well as to the side, and it can be performed as a double *frappé:* the working foot passes in front and behind (or vice versa) the supporting ankle before it brushes outward.

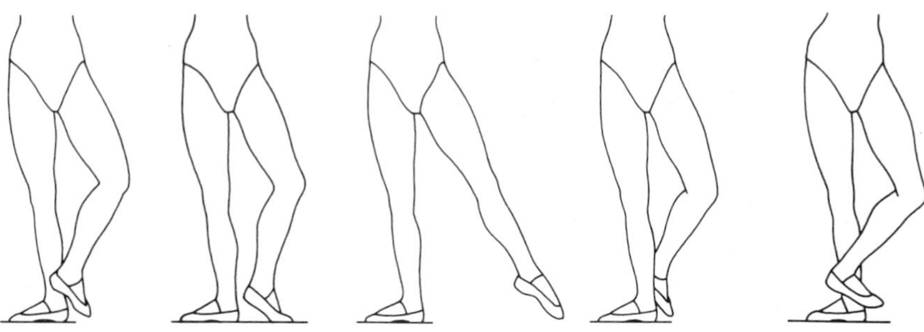

Battement frappé à la seconde Incorrect position

PETIT BATTEMENT SUR LE COU-DE-PIED
(p'TEE baht-MAH*n* suir l' koo-duh-pee-AY)

Definition: *Petit battement sur le cou-de-pied* means, literally, "small beat on the neck of the foot."

Purpose: The exercise is important in developing speed and precision in movement, particularly for *allegro* steps with beats.

Description: The exercise begins with the working foot placed at the ankle of the supporting foot. (The exact position of *sur le cou-de-pied* varies in different schools of technique—the foot may be "wrapped" around the ankle, heel in front and toes in back; it may be extended downward along the side of the ankle; it may be fully pointed in front or in back of the ankle; or it may be relaxed, heel touching the ankle and all five toes on the floor in *demi-pointe* position.) The *battements* consist of small, rapid out-and-in movements of the working foot around the supporting ankle.

Cautions: The thigh of the working leg does not move throughout the exercise, nor does the shape of the foot change as it goes from front to back (and vice versa) of the supporting ankle. The knee of the working leg remains relaxed so that the action can happen in the lower leg only.

Suggestions: To sense the quality of moving the lower leg freely from the knee joint: Stand sideways to the *barre* with the legs in parallel position, flex the outside leg so that the ball of the foot rests lightly on the floor, and place the free hand on the raised thigh. Keep the thigh immobile and the knee relaxed as the lower leg swings evenly forward and back. Next, perform this exercise with a turnout, allowing the working foot to swing evenly across in front and in back of the supporting foot. Later, speed is increased and accents can be added (back, *front*, hold; back, *front*, hold; etc.).

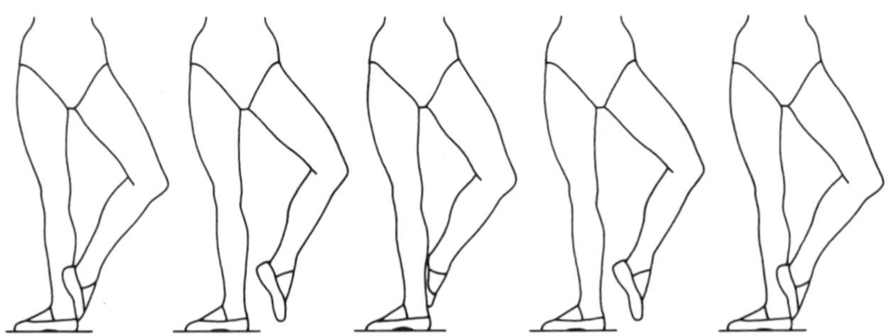

Petit battement sur le cou-de-pied

CIRCULAR MOVEMENTS

Circular movements of the leg, either along the ground or in the air, are important elements of *barre* work, later incorporated into exercises in center floor as well.

ROND DE JAMBE À TERRE (roh*n* duh zhah*n*b ah TAIR)

Definition: There are over a dozen exercises bearing the general term *rond de jambe* (literally, "circle or round of the leg"). The most basic is *rond de jambe à terre* (or *par terre*), the working leg describing a semicircle on the ground. When the foot travels in an arc from the front to the back, it is called an "outward" (*en dehors*) *rond de jambe.* When it travels from the back to the front, it is called an "inward" (*en dedans*) *rond de jambe.*

Purpose: In *ronds de jambe* the muscles and ligaments of the hip are exercised to allow the leg to move freely in a circular motion without disturbing the immobility of the torso. Characteristics of this movement are found in such steps as *pas de basque.*

Description: For *ronds de jambe en dehors,* slide the working foot forward from first position in the same way as *battement tendu* to the front, carry the toes in an arc along the ground through *pointe tendue à la seconde* to *pointe tendue* behind first position. Then bring the foot forward to first position in the same way as the closing of a *battement tendu.* (The direction of the entire exercise is reversed for a *rond de jambe en dedans.*)

Cautions: The toes of the working foot must remain in contact with the floor during the entire exercise. The working foot must remain fully arched as it traces the arc of the semicircle, taking care not to shorten the arc near the *pointes tendues* positions to the front or to the back. As the working foot passes through first position, it should relax but take care not to roll. Both legs must remain perfectly straight throughout the exercise. The supporting leg must resist any temptation to rotate inward, thus defeating one purpose of *rond de jambe:* improvement of turnout.

Suggestions: The *rond de jambe* is best learned slowly, with a pause in each position of the arc (front, side, back) and at the first position. Later, it usually is done to a 3/4 rhythm, with an entire semicircle completed during one measure, and a series of *ronds de jambe* executed without pause.

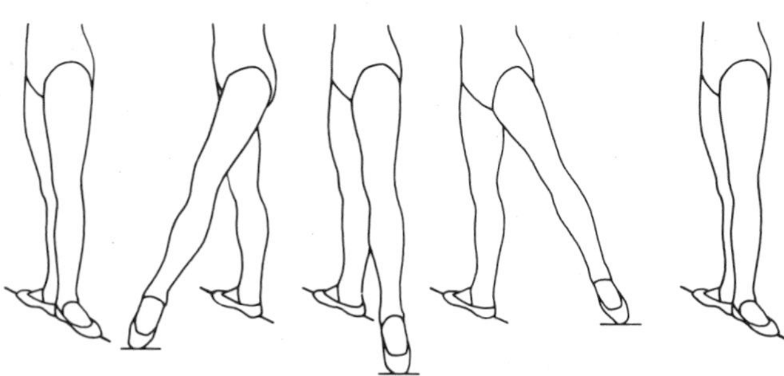

Rond de jambe à terre en dehors

DEMI-ROND DE JAMBE À LA DEMI-HAUTEUR

(duh-mee ROH*n* duh zhah*n*b ah la duh-mee oh-tuhr)

Definition: In the *demi-rond de jambe à la demi-hauteur*, the leg describes a quarter of a circle (usually from front to side, or from back to side) at half-height (forty-five degrees) in the air.

Purpose: As a preliminary exercise to more advanced *rond de jambe* series, this exercise introduces the important pelvic adjustments necessary for the leg to travel in the air from one direction to another. Strength, control, and coordination are the goals.

Description: From first or fifth position, brush the working foot either forward or backward as in a *battement dégagé*, but allow the leg to rise to forty-five degrees, and then open the leg *à la seconde* at the same level. Lower the leg until the toes touch at *pointe tendue à la seconde*, and slide the foot into the closed position.

Demi-rond de jambe à la demi-hauteur en dehors

and *en dedans*

Cautions: Although the movement of the open leg is the signature action, it is no more important than the active position of the supporting leg, which must be strongly extended and turned out throughout the exercise. Neither should the moving leg affect the straight alignment of the shoulders. The pelvis, however, will tilt slightly forward to allow the leg to rise to forty-five degrees to the back. It will then return to its normal upright position as the leg travels from the back to the side.

Suggestions: Coordination of breath and arm movements is helpful: Center the hand of the outside arm in front of the torso as the leg extends forward or backward, inhale, and raise the hand overhead as the leg moves *à la seconde*, thus increasing the upward stretch of the body and allowing greater freedom for the leg to make its circular movement. Open the arm outward to the side and lower it as the leg returns to the closed position.

ADDITIONAL BASIC EXERCISES

Out of the multitude of possible exercises to be included in *barre* work, only four more are given here. Again, the reader is reminded that no "proper" order of exercises has been implied in this chapter. Rather, exercises have been grouped according to general characteristics, with the following exercises sharing a folding-and-unfolding design for the leg or for the torso.

BATTEMENT RETIRÉ (baht-MAH*n* ruh-tih-RAY)

Definition: The *battement retiré* is a "withdrawing" of the working foot from the floor until it touches the front, side, or back of the supporting knee. The term *passé* is sometimes used when the foot passes from fifth position front to fifth position back and vice versa.

Purpose: This exercise is an integral part of many movements in ballet, such as *développés* and *pas de chats.* It has great value in warming up the thighs and in strengthening the muscles in the waist and back. *Retirés* (or *passés*) also can improve balance and turnout.

Description: For the simplest *retiré,* the working foot is raised from first position until the toes touch the hollow at the side of the supporting knee, thus lifting the thigh to a well turned-out second position *en l'air* (in the air). The foot then returns to the closed position.

Cautions: The working foot should push off from the floor so that the movement of the *retiré* is crisp. The thigh of the working leg must be well turned out and the foot in correct alignment (not "sickled"). The heel of the working foot must never touch the knee of the supporting leg. When the foot returns to the closed position, it should "roll down" as it touches the floor; that is, the toes should touch first, then the ball of the foot, the sole, and lastly the heel.

Suggestions: After mastering *battements retirés* from first position, practice them from third or fifth position and then passing them from front to back, and vice versa. Later still, the exercises may be taken from a *demi-plié* to a *relevé,* with a return to *demi-plié.* These basic exercises, and their many variations, can first be learned facing the *barre.*

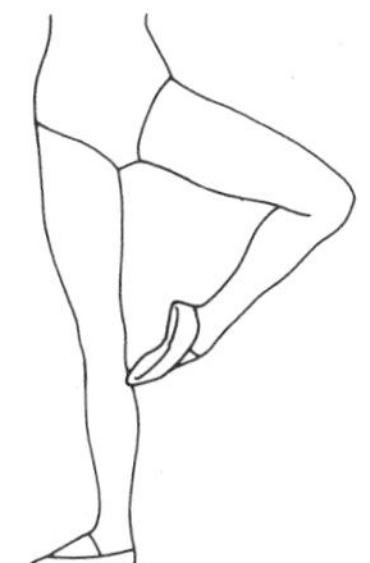

Retiré

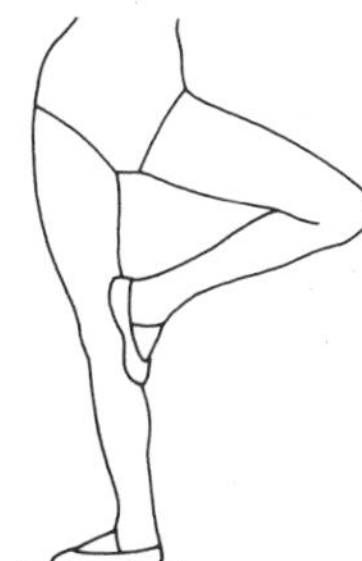

Incorrect *retiré*

DÉVELOPPÉ (day-vloh-PAY)

Definition: In the *développé,* the working foot is drawn up to the supporting knee and then the leg is "developed" (unfolded) to an open position at forty-five or ninety degrees in the air in any given direction.

Purpose: This is one of the most fundamental exercises of *adagio* (the slow, sustained movements of ballet), for it is the method by which the leg can arrive at many ballet positions, such as *arabesque. Développés,* done repeatedly as an exercise, have great strengthening value for the muscles of the abdomen, legs, and back.

Description: For a *développé à la seconde,* the working foot is drawn up along the side of the supporting leg to the *retiré* position, then unfolded to second position *en l'air.* The leg also can be developed to the front or to the back. Different ballet styles may prefer the working leg to unfold from a position in front of or behind the supporting knee rather than from the side of the knee.

Cautions: The working foot must be arched as soon as it leaves the closed position, and it must travel close to the supporting leg until it reaches the knee. The working leg must remain well turned out as it opens to the extended position. Correct placement (especially of the hips) must never be sacrificed for a high extension.

Suggestions: First master the control and balance necessary for the *retiré* before attempting the *développé.* Ideally, the *développé* should be done slowly and smoothly in one continuous flow from the closed position to the extended position. Nevertheless, it is helpful to practice the exercise with slight pauses of the foot, first at the ankle, then at the knee, then at the halfway position before full extension, and finally at the full height of the *développé.* The leg should be lowered slowly to *pointe tendue,* and returned to the closed position. It is best first to learn the leg movements alone before adding coordinated arm movements.

Développé à la seconde

BATTEMENT FONDU (baht-MAH*n* foh*n*-DIU)

Definition: *Battement fondu* ("sinking down") is a compound exercise consisting of a bending and straightening of the supporting leg and a *développé* of the other leg.

Purpose: The basic action of *battement fondu*—the coordination of bending and straightening the legs—is inherent in practically every *allegro* step, as well as in many *adagio* movements. It is especially essential for jumps, as it exercises all the muscles of the legs needed in jumping. When done to the *demi-pointe*, it exercises the foot also.

Description: As the foot of the working leg comes to a pointed position either in front of or behind the supporting ankle, the supporting leg bends, with the supporting heel remaining firmly on the floor. The *développé* of the working leg occurs simultaneously with the straightening of the supporting leg, and then both legs bend at the same time to begin the exercise again.

Cautions: The *battement fondu* should be done smoothly without pauses at any stage. Care must be taken that both legs remain turned out throughout the exercise. Because the exercise is very strenuous, it should not be repeated a great number of times.

Suggestions: Do not attempt the *battement fondu* until the more elementary *barre* exercises have been mastered. In the first attempt, the unfolding of the working leg should be limited to the position of *pointe tendue à la seconde.* Later it can be unfolded to an angle of forty-five degrees, then to ninety degrees to the front and back as well as to the side. Only after the basic *fondu* is mastered should the exercise include a *relevé* on the supporting foot.

Battement fondu à la seconde

PORT DE BRAS AU CORPS CAMBRÉ
(por duh BRAH oh kor kah*n*-BRAY)

Definition: *Port de bras au corps cambré* means, literally, "carriage of the arms with an arched body." Usually the term is used to describe the bending of the body backward or sideward from the waist. The forward bend from the hips is sometimes termed *penché*, or simply *port de bras* forward.

Purpose: Ballet technique is more than legwork. This exercise is important because it involves movement of the head, arms, and torso, and not, as in all other *barre* exercises, the legs. It also limbers and relaxes the upper body and coordinates arm and head movements—all necessary for fluidity of motion.

Description: In the forward bend, the upper body bends from the hips until it is parallel to the floor, continuing forward until the torso is near the legs (the back may remain almost straight or may round over). Return to the upright position can be made by retracing the path of the forward bend or by "uncurling" (rolling up) through the spine. The bend backward begins with a lift in the chest as the face and one arm rise toward the ceiling, continuing into an arch backward (with the face toward the ceiling or turned slightly toward the center of the room). Return to the upright position can be made by retracing the path of the backward bend or by opening the arm to the side as the back straightens. The bend sideward occurs from the waist and is done with one arm raised over the top of the head and ribs well lifted. Return to the upright position can be made by retracing the path of the sideward bend or by bringing the arm forward and then to the side as the torso straightens.

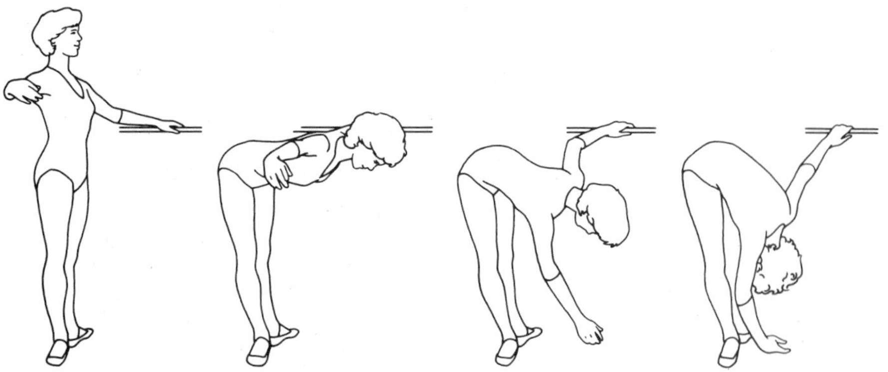

Port de bras forward

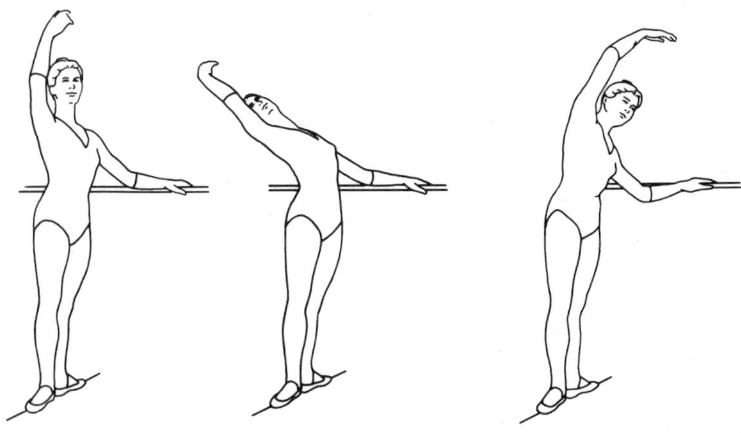

Cambré backward

Cambré sideward

Cautions: The legs must remain straight and the weight of the body evenly distributed on both feet when the exercises are done from any of the five positions. Do not push back on the heels or sway the back in the forward bend. Avoid straining the neck or shoulders and shortening the lower spine as the body bends backward. Alignment of the legs and hips should not alter as the torso bends in any direction. All movements must be done smoothly.

Suggestions: These bending exercises should be learned in first position before they are attempted in other positions. Learn the forward bend as a half-bend; that is, stretch forward until the upper body is parallel to the floor (or as parallel as possible, given the stretch in the legs) and then return to the upright position. The bend backward at first can be learned facing the *barre*. An intake of breath just before and during the bend is helpful.

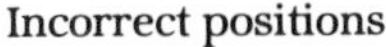

Incorrect positions

Weight pushed back, spine swayed

Knees bent, pelvis released

Torso twisted, weight off center

STRETCHES

Stretches are matters of some controversy among ballet teachers. There are those who advocate stretches and incorporate them into the classwork. Others feel that *barre* exercises alone give proper limbering, and that most other stretching exercises are artificial and useless ("If you are limber, stretches are unnecessary; if you aren't limber, stretches won't help!"). All would agree, however, that stretches should be attempted only when the body is thoroughly warmed up—after the completion of *barre* work, or at the end of class.

It is the author's opinion that certain stretches, if done correctly, are useful to certain bodies, but, for ballet, flexibility must be attained *along with* strength and endurance. Therefore, a few words of general advice are offered rather than an outline of specific limbering exercises.

Suggestions: Allow the body to relax into the stretch. Forceful bouncing or reaching, which causes one set of muscles to tighten as another set is stretched, defeats limbering. All stretches should be done slowly and smoothly. The correct position of the foot on the floor, the lift of the arch, and the alignment of foot with leg must not be sacrificed during stretches in a standing position. Do your own stretching. Relying on others to lift, to bend, or to push your limbs and torso can be dangerous. And, finally, do stretches only when the body is fully warmed up.

CHAPTER 4
BALLET TECHNIQUE: CENTER WORK

When *barre* work is completed, the mechanics of ballet technique are brought into the center floor. To the movements of the legs and feet now are added movements of the head, carriages of the arms (*ports de bras*), and positions of the shoulders (*épaulements*), which bring artistic life to even the simplest ballet exercise. Using all these elements—the entire body—to create harmonious designs in space is the challenge of center work.

DIRECTIONS OF THE STUDIO/STAGE

Ballet is taught as a performing art, even though ninety-nine percent of all ballet students may never set foot on a professional stage. Positions and movements of center floor work are based on the assumption that an audience is at the front of the room. At all times the dancer/student must be aware of body line in relation to the eye of that audience. The parts of the stage have directional names that are useful in the studio: *Downstage* is toward the audience. *Upstage* is away from the audience. *Stage right* is to the dancer's right as the dancer faces the audience. *Stage left* is then to the dancer's left. These directional names remain constant, no matter which way the dancer faces.

Much of beginning work is done facing the "audience" (a direction known as *de face*, although movement made toward the audience often is said to be done *en face*). When asked to face a corner direction, students should first imagine themselves standing in the center of a "private" stage about a yard square, then face the corner of that square, rather than the actual corner of the studio, and, from the neck downward, align the body with the downstage corner of that

Downstage left | Audience Downstage | Downstage right

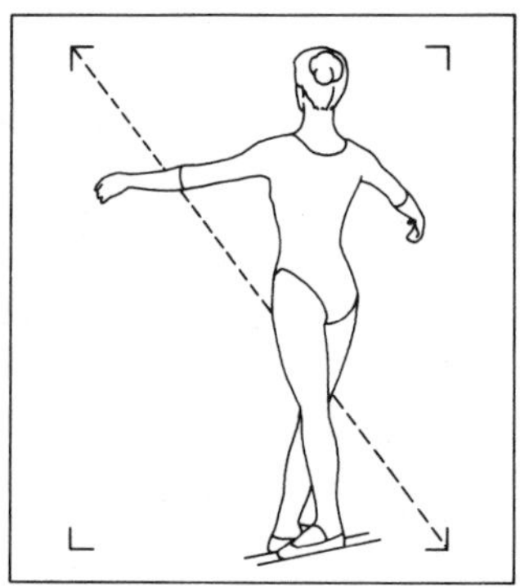

Upstage left | Upstage | Upstage right

imaginary stage square. For practicing movements of the arms and positions of the body, a thirty-six-inch square, complete with diagonals (as in the diagram above), can be outlined on the floor with masking tape. Do not, however, imagine solid walls around the small square, for the poses must never appear tight or static. Even the stillness of the body must look alive, as though the limbs might grow beyond the confines of the studio walls or ceiling.

POSITIONS OF THE ARMS

The positions of the arms correspond to the positions of the feet. However, no rule says that if the feet are in fifth position, the arms must always be in a particular position. Some variation occurs in the numbering and naming of the basic arm positions in different teaching methods. It is pointless to argue over numbers or names; learn those used in your school and concentrate on the desired shape of the arms. Although there are slight variations in the style of the positions, the following general rules of form can be helpful for most basic positions: The arms should curve gently from shoulder to fingertip, eliminating the pointed look of the elbows. The hands should be held simply, the wrists neither stiff nor floppy, the fingers curved and only slightly separated, with the thumb and middle finger brought close together. In the middle positions, either to the front or to the side, the arms may have a gradual slope downward from the shoulders to the elbows, then to the wrists, and finally to the fingers. The arms should move freely from the shoulder sockets (not from the elbows), but the shoulders must remain in place. When the hand is over the head, it should be just within the line of vision as the performer looks straight forward.

The following descriptions and illustrations represent only one of several possibilities for terminology, style, and numbering of arm positions; others are equally valid.

Basic positions in which the arms and hands are to the side of the body and, usually, just slightly forward:

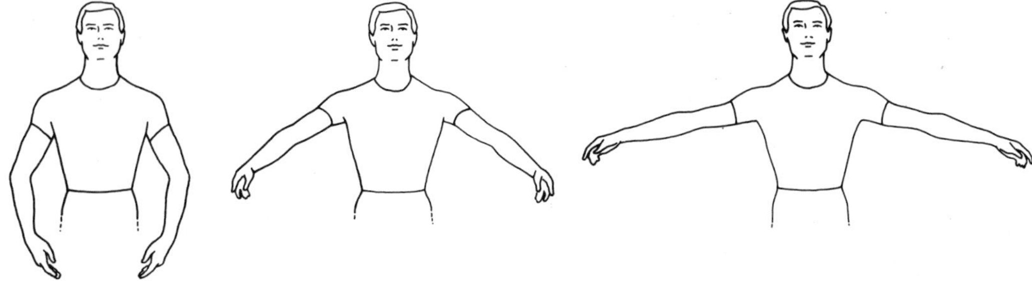

First (preparatory) *Demi-seconde* Second (*à la seconde*)

Basic positions in which the hands are centered on the body, only a few inches apart, the arms forming an oval shape:

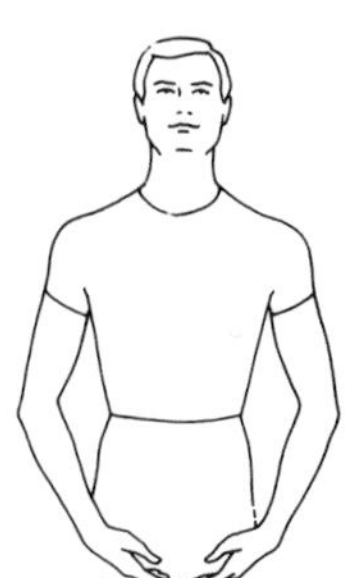

Bras bas (en bas)
(arms low)

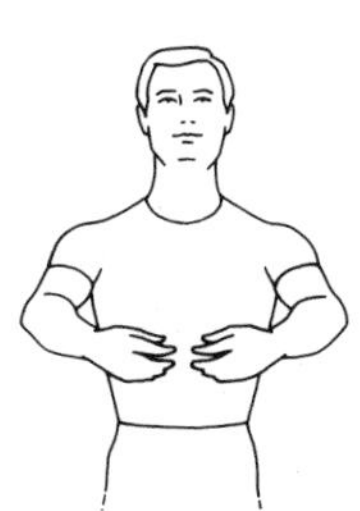

Bras avant (en avant)
(arms forward)

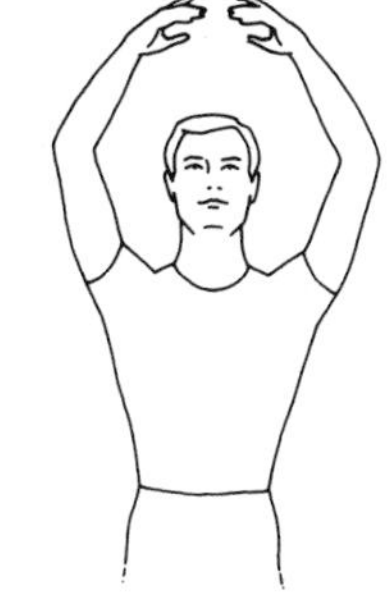

Bras hauts (en haut)
(arms high)

Possible variations of these basic positions, which have a variety of different names and numbers, include:

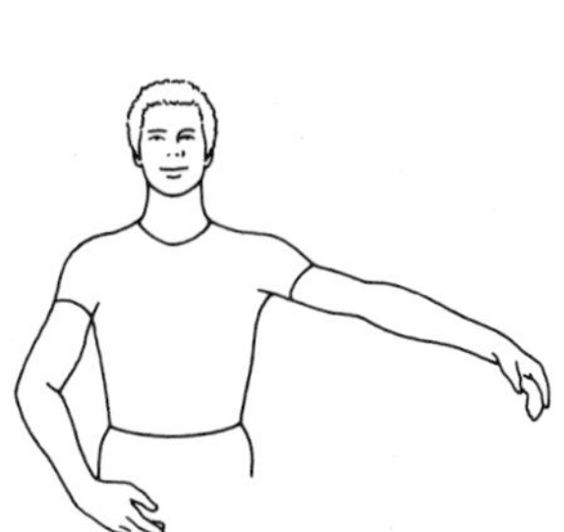

POSITIONS OF THE HEAD

During *barre* work in beginning classes, the position of the head seldom varies. It is held regally on a long neck, with chin parallel to the floor and eyes looking (not staring) straight forward. This attitude sets the tone for the elegant style of ballet, but in center work the head must learn to move in harmony with the rest of the body. Five different positions of the head can be used:

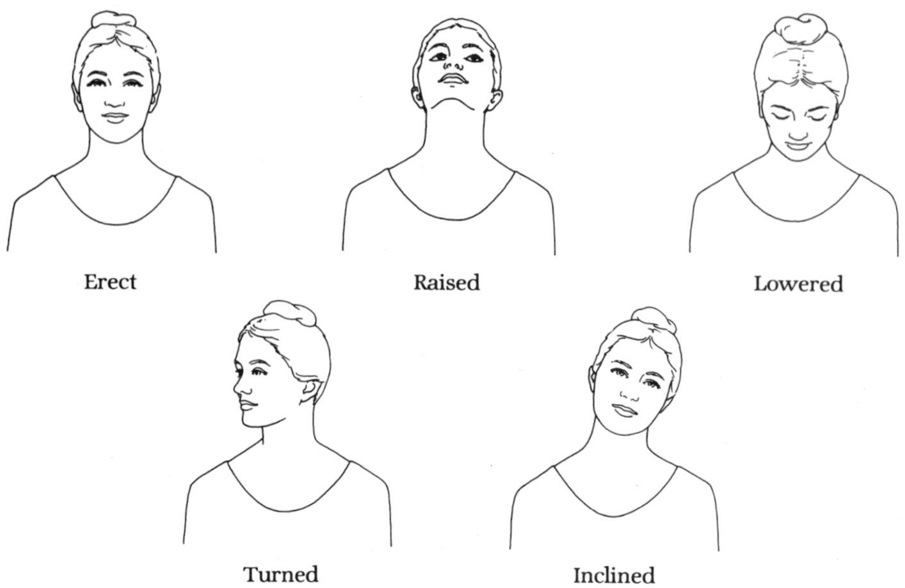

Erect Raised Lowered

Turned Inclined

These positions can be combined, for instance:

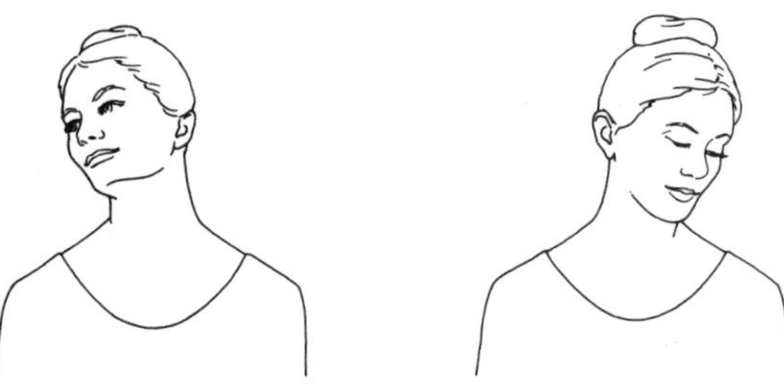

Turned and inclined Lowered and turned

PORT DE BRAS (por duh BRAH)

Center floor work often begins with *port de bras,* which refers not only to arm movements but to groups of exercises for the arms. The earlier term *corps et bras* ("body and arms") remains a more descriptive title, because, in these exercises, the head, shoulders, and torso are very much involved (even though the legs often can enjoy a rest).

An infinite variety of *ports de bras* is possible within the basic framework provided by the positions of the arms. There are, however, two set exercises of the arms that are most fundamental and used most often with *adagio* and *allegro* movements. They look deceptively simple, but, in the words of Vaganova, "*Port de bras* is the most difficult part of the dance, requiring the greatest amount of work and concentration."[1]

Again, variations of style exist, but the following descriptions outline two basic exercises:

Exercise 1

1. The starting pose: Face downstage left in third or fifth position (right foot front), the arms *en bas*, the head inclined to the left and slightly lowered.

Exercise 1

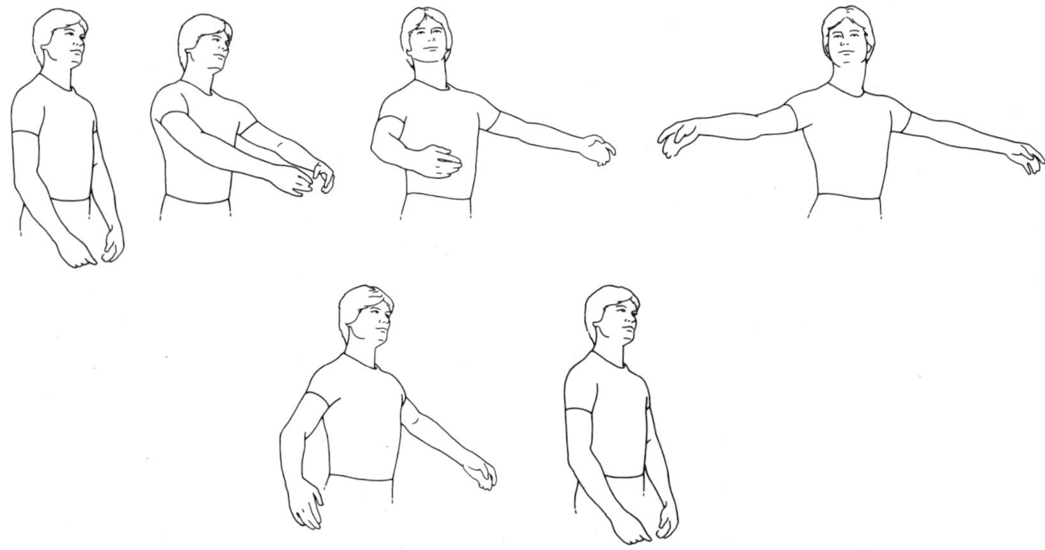

2. Raise the arms *en avant* and, at the same time, lean the torso slightly forward from the waist.
3. Open the palms slightly and carry both arms to second position while the head turns and inclines to the right. During this movement the torso can also lean to the right a small degree, and the eyes follow in the direction of the right hand. The hips and shoulders do not twist but remain in alignment facing the original downstage corner.
4. Lower the arms to the starting pose as the head simultaneously returns to its original position.

Exercise 2

1. The starting pose: the same as in Exercise 1.
2. Raise the arms *en avant* as the torso inclines slightly forward and the head remains inclined to the left.
3. Continue to raise the arms *en haut* while the torso straightens and the head lifts and then inclines to the right.
4. Open both arms to second position as the torso leans slightly to the right and the eyes follow in the direction of the right hand. The hips and shoulders do not twist.
5. Lower the arms to the starting pose as the head simultaneously returns to its original position.

Exercise 2

Each *port de bras* is done several times in succession, and each sequence is practiced to the other side as well. Traditionally, most center exercises that are done diagonally begin toward the downstage left corner. Exercises are done slowly and smoothly so that the movement flows through, but does not stop, in

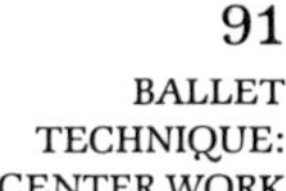

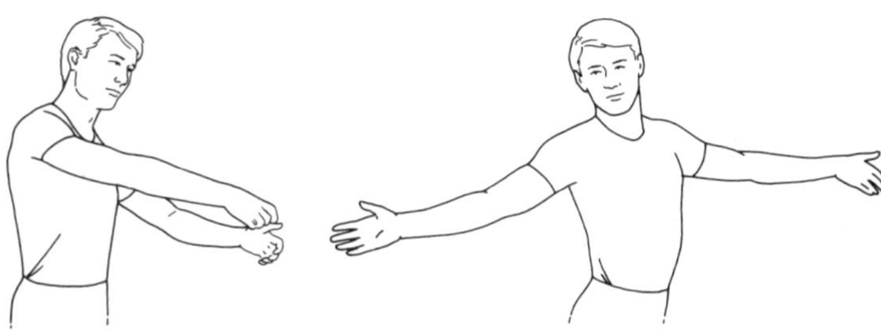

Incorrect

any one position. Take care that the hands stay centered on the body as they travel from the *bras bas* position to *bras hauts*, that the shoulders do not rise or twist, and that the fingers do not spread open.

This brief discussion of *port de bras* ends with a further observation from Vaganova: "Only the ability to find the proper position for her arms lends a finesse to the artistic expression of the dancer, and renders full harmony to her dance. The head gives it the finishing touch, adds beauty to the entire design. The look, the glance, the eyes, crown it all."[2]

CENTER EXERCISES AND *ÉPAULEMENT* (ay-pohl-MAH*n*)

Center work includes a repetition of numerous *barre* exercises without the aid of the *barre*. Because these *exercises au milieu* (eg-zehr-SEESS oh mee-LYUH) are often done on alternate feet, they can help develop greater balance, coordination, and control.

An example is a series of *battements tendus* traveling forward: From fifth position right foot back, *battement tendu à la seconde* with the right foot, closing front in fifth position; repeat with the left foot. Continue in this way, alternating right and left legs eight or sixteen times.

The exercise is then reversed so that the *battements tendus* close in fifth position back. Beginning students generally practice these and similar exercises *de face*—that is, directly toward the front of the room. Later an important embellishment is added, enlivening an otherwise flat appearance. It is called *épaulement*. Although this literally means "shouldering," it encompasses movement of the head and upper body as well as the shoulders. The traditional rule for *épaulement* is: In steps that travel forward, the head and shoulders are aligned with the foot that closes front, the head turning slightly toward the working foot. In steps that travel backward, the head and shoulders are in opposition to the foot that closes back, the head inclining slightly away from the working foot.

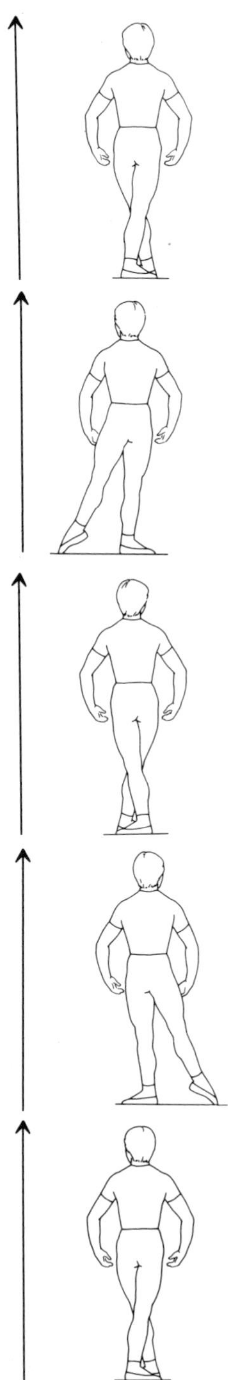

Therefore, the exercise of *battements tendus* traveling forward using *épaulement* is: From fifth position right foot in back, extend the right foot *à la seconde* and, simultaneously, bring the right shoulder slightly forward of the left, with the head slightly turned to the right. The head and right shoulder are now aligned with the right or working foot. Close to fifth position front without changing the *épaulement.* The exercise is repeated with the left leg, so that the left shoulder is brought forward, and the head is turned to the left.

The exercise of *battements tendus* traveling backward with *épaulement* is: From fifth position left foot in front, extend the left foot *à la seconde* and, simultaneously, bring the right shoulder slightly forward of the left, with the head slightly inclined to the right. The head and right shoulder are now in opposition to the left or working foot. Close to fifth position behind without changing the *épaulement.* The exercise continues alternating legs, the shoulders and head always in opposition to the working leg.

The degree and style of *épaulement* used is a matter of preference, but the following general rules should always be observed: The hips face directly front and do not turn or twist when the *épaulement* is taken. The shoulders are not raised as they are brought into alignment or opposition.

Épaulement is not confined to center exercises. The principles of alignment and opposition are used constantly in *adagio* phrases, which are done later in the center. The final stage of instruction, the *allegro,* includes many steps that are improved greatly by the addition of a little shouldering action. However, the student should have a solid understanding of the mechanics of these steps before embellishing them with *épaulement.*

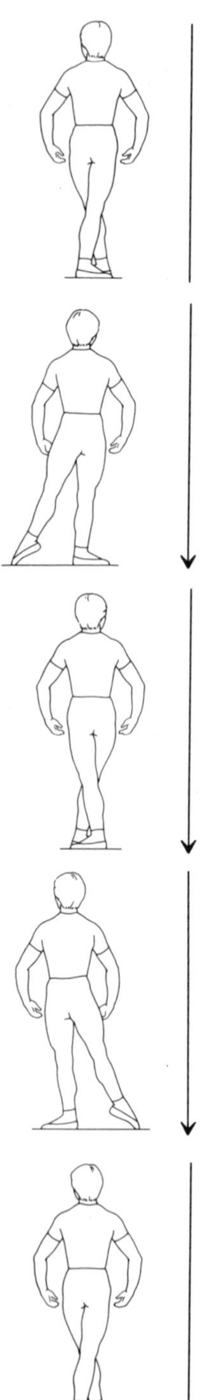

Traveling forward

Traveling backward

POSITIONS OF THE BODY

The classic line of ballet is built on the alignment of the body in space, as well as on alignment within the body. There are eleven positions of the body in space, from which infinite variations of poses are possible. Frequently, eight of these positions are practiced in a specific sequence as a center floor exercise. They are learned first with the extended leg at *pointe tendue;* later, with the leg raised to forty-five degrees, and then to ninety degrees. One common sequence for these positions is shown here, illustrated as though seen from the back so that the reader may relate to the positions more easily.

FACING FRONT

Beginning students quite soon are familiar with the three positions of the body that face directly front (*en face*), or toward the audience:

À la quatrième devant (ah la ka-tree-EHM duh-VAH*n*): The extended leg is in fourth position front; the arms are in second position; the head, hips, and shoulders face directly front.

À la quatrième derrière (deh-reeAIR): The extended leg is in fourth position back; the arms are in second position; the head, hips, and shoulders face directly front.

À la seconde (ah la suh-GOH*n*D): The extended leg is in second position; the arms are in second position; the head, hips, and shoulders face directly front.

ON THE DIAGONAL

Once the front-facing positions are mastered, the student is introduced to poses on the diagonal. The terms for these poses, translated literally, are: *croisé* ("crossed"), *effacé* ("shaded"), *écarté* ("separated" or "thrown wide apart"), and *épaulé* ("shouldered"). The following descriptions reflect the author's preference in style; other variations are equally valid:

Croisé (krawh-ZAY) *devant:* The dancer faces either downstage corner; the leg nearer the audience extends to fourth position front; the arm opposite the extended leg is *en haut* and the other arm is *demi-seconde;* the torso and head incline slightly toward the low arm.

Croisé derrière: The dancer faces either downstage corner; the leg farther from the audience extends to fourth position back; the arm opposite the extended leg is *en haut* and the other arm is *demi-seconde;* the head and torso incline very slightly toward the low arm so that the dancer appears to be looking at the audience from under the high arm.

Effacé (eh-fah-SAY) *devant:* The dancer faces either downstage corner; the

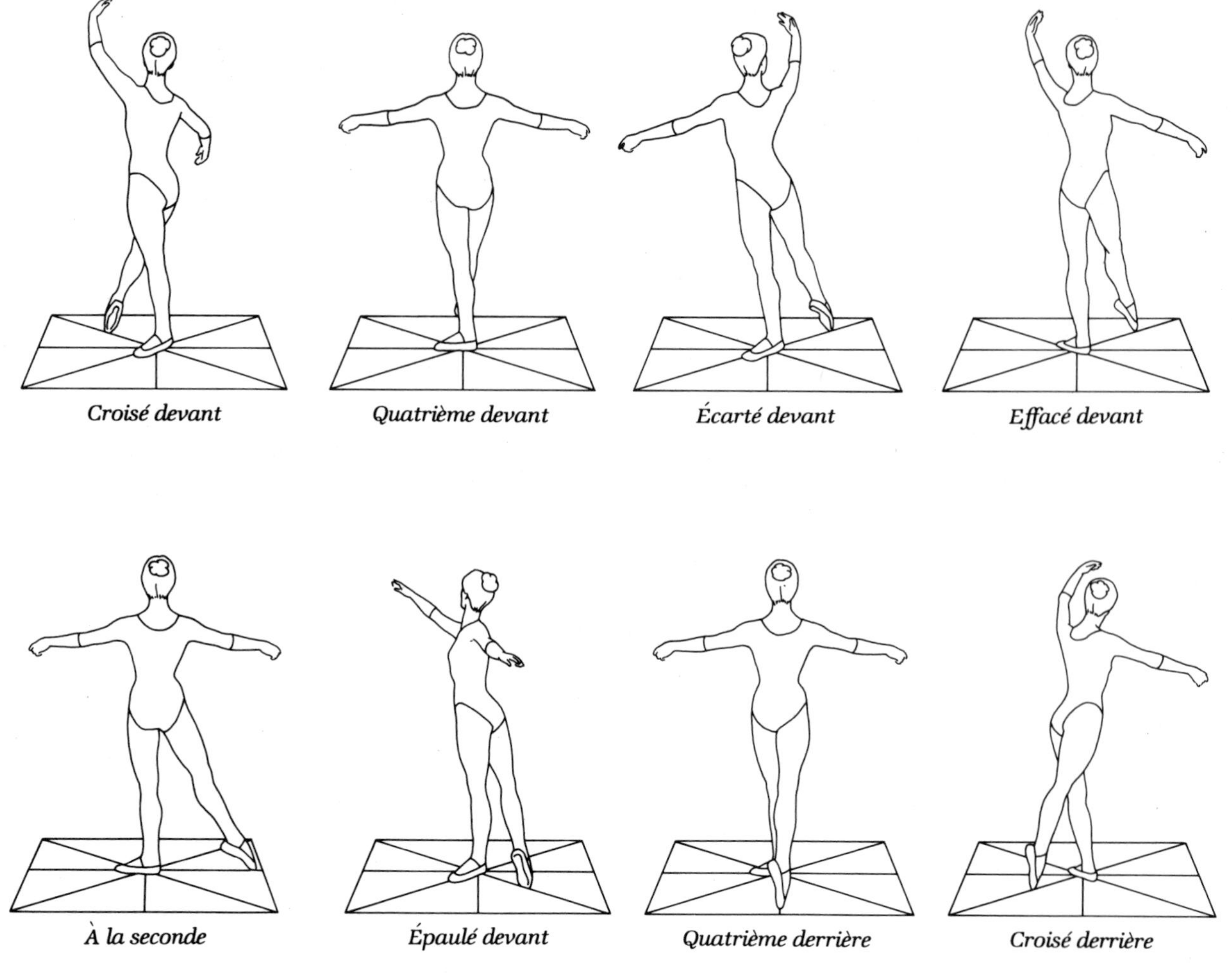

Croisé devant | *Quatrième devant* | *Écarté devant* | *Effacé devant*

À la seconde | *Épaulé devant* | *Quatrième derrière* | *Croisé derrière*

leg farther from the audience extends to fourth position front; the arm opposite the extended leg is *en haut* and the other arm is *demi-seconde*; the body leans very slightly back from the waist and the head inclines toward the high arm.

Effacé derrière: The dancer faces either downstage corner; the leg nearer the the audience extends to fourth position back; the arm on the same side as the extended leg is *en haut* and the other arm is *demi-seconde*; the body leans slightly forward over the supporting foot; the head turns and rises slightly toward the hand that is high.

Écarté (ay-kar-TAY) *devant*: The dancer faces either downstage corner; the leg nearer the audience extends to second position; the arm on the same side as the extended leg is *en haut* and the other arm is *demi-seconde*; the torso is erect; the head turns and rises slightly toward the hand that is high.

Écarté derrière: The dancer faces either downstage corner; the leg farther from the audience extends to second position; the arm on the same side as the extended leg is *en haut* and the other arm is *demi-seconde;* the torso and head incline slightly toward the hand that is low.

Épaulé (ay-poh-LAY) *devant:* The dancer faces either downstage corner; the leg nearer the audience extends to fourth position back; the arm nearer the audience extends forward and the other arm extends backward; the torso turns slightly from the waist so that the back arm is visible to the audience; the head inclines toward the front shoulder. (This position corresponds to second *arabesque*, see page 97, except that it is taken toward the corner instead of in profile.)

Épaulé derrière: This position is exactly the same as *épaulé devant*, except that the dancer faces either of the upstage corners.

OTHER POSES OF THE BODY

Attitude and *arabesque* are two poses most frequently associated with ballet. As the reader readily can imagine by now, variations of these poses are practically unlimited and differences of style do exist. Still, certain fundamental rules remain constant.

ATTITUDE (ah-tee-TEWD)

The ballet *attitude* is a pose on one leg, the other leg lifted, well turned out and bent at the knee with the foot opened away from the body. Carlo Blasis, an early nineteenth-century ballet master and author of important dance technique manuals, considered the *attitude* to be the most elegant but, at the same time, the most difficult pose in dancing. He believed it to be a kind of imitation of the statue of Mercury, messenger of the gods, by the artist Giovanni da Bologna.[3] However, in today's technique, unlike in the Renaissance statue, the bent knee is lifted, well turned out, and level with, or higher than, the raised foot.

When the leg is lifted to the back, the pose is known as *attitude derrière.* Another variation calls for the leg to be lifted to the front, well turned out, the knee bent, and the foot raised as high as possible. This pose is known as *attitude devant.*

Mercury — *Attitude croisée derrière* — *Attitude croisée devant*

Attitudes can be done in many positions of the body, although most commonly in *croisé* or *effacé* positions. Usually one arm is raised *en haut* and the other opened *à la seconde*, but variations are introduced, usually in later training.

ARABESQUE (ah-ra-BESK)

Perhaps the "ultimate" pose in today's ballet is the *arabesque*, in which the body is balanced over one foot with the other leg fully extended behind. The arms also are extended, palms down, creating a long, symmetrical line from fingertips to toetips. Blasis surmised that the design and name were derived from ancient paintings, which in turn had been influenced by the Moorish and Arabic taste for architectural ornaments and embellishments.[4]

Arabesques are learned *à terre*—that is, the toes of the extended leg touching the ground. Later, as the leg is gradually raised to ninety degrees, the torso is allowed to lean slightly forward, but the back must remain well arched, the muscles of the waist held strongly, and the weight of the body shifted well forward over the ball of the supporting foot. The lifted leg must be well turned out from the hip, which causes a slight rotation in the lower spine. The arms in *arabesque* are extended, not curved, with the fingers also extended and the palms facing the floor. At all times, the height of the arms must balance the height of the leg, enabling an unbroken line to be drawn from the fingers of the front hand to the toes of the extended foot.

Three basic *arabesques* are given here. The extended leg is pictured at different levels, *à terre* to ninety degrees, any of which may be done in any of the *arabesques.*

First *arabesque:* The dancer stands in profile to the audience; the leg nearer the audience extends to the back; the forward arm corresponds to the supporting leg; the other arm is taken slightly back of second position but without strain to the shoulder; the eyes focus over the forward hand.

Second *arabesque:* The dancer stands as in first *arabesque,* except the arms are reversed so that the forward arm is in opposition to the supporting leg; the shoulders turn, allowing the back arm to be visible; the head inclines toward the audience.

Third *arabesque* (or *arabesque à deux bras*): The dancer stands as in first *arabesque*, but with both arms extended forward; the arm farther from the audience is slightly higher; the focus is to the higher hand.

These three *arabesques* can be taken toward the downstage diagonal direction, rather than in profile to the audience. In these variations, the supporting leg is sometimes bent (*en fondu*).

A common pose in later training is *arabesque penchée* (pah*n*-SHAY), in which the leg is raised very high, causing the torso to lean well forward. The head and forward arm are low, counterbalancing the raised foot, which is the highest point of the pose.

TURNS

Most poses and steps can be done *en tournant*, or turning. They at once become more exciting to watch and more challenging to perform. Probably no aspect of ballet has received more analysis by teachers (or attention by students) than the *pirouette*, a complete spin on one foot.

Any turn demands a correctly aligned body whose feet, legs, and back have been strengthened by elementary ballet exercises. To this strong vertical balance is added the first principle of turning—the quick snap of the head, called *spotting*.

SPOTTING

For a turn in place, the gaze stays momentarily on a fixed point straight in front of the body as the turn begins. The head then leads the turn, arriving back at the fixed focal point before the rest of the body. This manipulation of the head allows the dancer to turn without becoming dizzy, and it contributes to the momentum for fast turns. The origin of the trick of spotting is not known. Erik Bruhn, a fine dancer who turns quite naturally, suggests that it perhaps was "originally an accidental discovery which some dancer later embodied in his teaching and which eventually became a universally accepted practice."[5]

Practice

Students who find turning less than second nature (and there are many who do) can become acquainted with spotting by revolving slowly in place while taking small steps on both feet. The head should remain momentarily on a fixed point to the front and then snap around to finish the revolution before the rest of the body. The head is erect, and the fixed focal point is on a line level with the eyes.

Spotting for turns

TURNS ON TWO FEET

Once the principle of spotting is understood, the student practices turns on two feet. These are done in place as *soutenus en tournant*, or traveling as *chaînés* and *tours de basque.*

SOUTENU EN TOURNANT (soo-teh-NEW ah*n* toor-NAN*n*)

Definition: Meaning "sustained turning," this movement most commonly is executed *en dedans*, or inwards.

Description: From fifth position, left foot back, slide the left foot to the side while bending the right knee. Draw the left foot straight in to fifth position front while simultaneously rising to the *demi-pointes* and turning right, thus facing the back of the room. (The left foot will be in front of the right.) Continue turning to the right on both feet until facing the front of the room once more, leaving the left foot in back in fifth position. The turn also is called *assemblé soutenu en tournant en dedans*, which implies a slight spring to the *demi-pointe* position. Reverse the movements to perform the turn *en dehors.*

Suggestions: The leg that opens and closes must stay straight. Open the arms to second position as the foot goes to second; close the arms *en avant* or *en haut*, keeping the hands centered on the body, as the turn is made.

Soutenu en tournant en dedans

Preparatory Exercises

The mechanics of these turns can be practiced at the *barre* as simple *battements soutenus:* Slide one foot *à la seconde* while the supporting leg bends; close in fifth position either *à terre* (heels on the ground) or *en relevé*. Later, half-turns can be practiced at the *barre* and in center, and, finally, the complete turn can be done in center.

CHAÎNÉS (sheh-NAY)

Definition: *Chaînés* ("chains, links") are a succession of rapid, traveling turns. They are also called *déboulés* ("rolling like a ball").

Description: *Chaînés* are a series of small, very rapid steps done on *demi-pointes* with a half-turn on each step. They are done across the floor, usually on a diagonal line. Later, they can be performed in a circle around the studio (*en manège*).

Suggestions: Turn evenly on each foot, for it takes two half-turns to make one full *chaîné* turn. Do not fling the arms around; keep them stationary, usually *en bas* or *en avant*, or in first position. Keep the hips and shoulders aligned and the legs well turned out.

Preparatory Exercises

Make slow turning steps in second position, keeping the arms in second position for better balance. Concentrate on the spotting of the head toward a fixed point in the direction of the turns and on making *even* half-turns straight across the room. Later, turn with more speed, with the legs closer together (first position, heels almost touching), the arms low, and the path a diagonal from upstage left to downstage right, then from upstage right to downstage left. If balance is lost or proper direction cannot be maintained, walk quickly out of the line of traffic and, if possible, begin again.

TOUR DE BASQUE (toor duh BAHSK)

Definition: *Tour de basque* (literally, "Basque turn") is also known as *pas de basque sur les pointes* ("Basque step on the points"), reflecting a kinship with steps traditional to dances of the Basque people (see page 123).

Description: From fifth position, right foot front, brush the right foot slightly off the ground to the front and then open it out to the side (*demi-rond de jambe en l'air*) while bending the left leg. Immediately step (*piqué*) onto the right *demi-pointe* in second position and quickly close the left foot to fifth position front as the body makes one-half turn to the right. Continue turning to the right on both feet until facing the beginning direction once more, leaving the left foot in back in fifth position. Another turn can follow immediately to the same direction.

Suggestions: The crisp look of this turn is enhanced not only by the straight leg executing the *demi-rond de jambe* and *piqué,* but also by the strong push from the floor and quick close to fifth position front by the second foot. As in *soutenu en tournant,* this turn commences simultaneously with the closing to fifth position, aided by the brisk closing of both arms from second position to a low, middle, or high position.

Preparatory Exercises

Before trying the turn, practice just the *demi-rond de jambe* and *piqué* to second position, closing the second foot quickly to fifth position front. Repeat the exercise immediately to the other side.

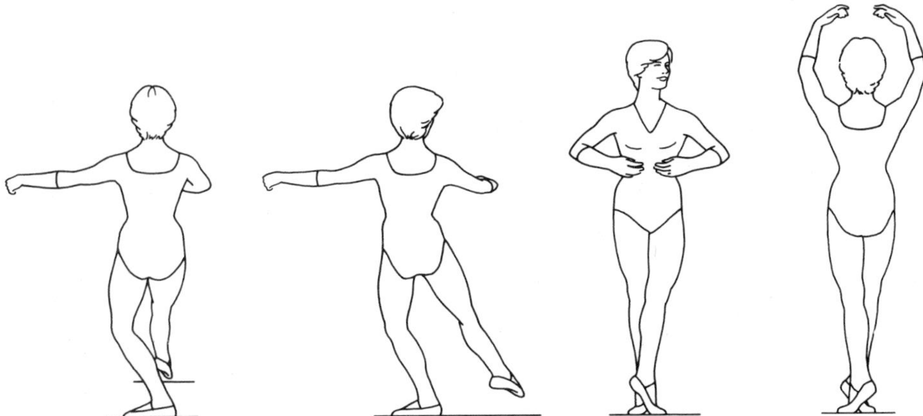

Tour de basque

TURNS ON ONE FOOT

Turns on one foot, such as *pirouettes,* are not included in most first-year classes, but exercises to help achieve the strength and form for them are.

PIROUETTES (peer-oo-ET)

Definition: A *pirouette* ("whirl, spin") is a complete turn of the body and is usually executed on the ball of the foot. The direction of the spin can be *en dehors* (turning outward in the direction of the raised leg) or *en dedans* (turning inward in the direction of the supporting leg).

Preparatory Exercises

Practice for *pirouettes en dehors* can include a series of *relevés* taken from *demi-pliés* in second, fourth, or fifth positions onto the *demi-pointe* of one foot. The other foot, strongly pointed and turned out, is placed somewhere between the ankle and the knee of the supporting leg, depending on the preference of the particular school. These *relevés* are practiced facing the *barre,* with time allowed for balancing on the *demi-pointe.* Later, preparatory exercises in center floor can coordinate movements of the arms with the legs. For instance, *demi-plié* in fifth position, right foot front, the right arm curved forward of the body (*en avant*) and the left arm open to second position. With a push from both heels, *relevé* onto the left foot as the open arm joins the other *en avant,* hands close together and slightly below the chest. After the balance in this position, the feet can return to fifth position *demi-plié* as the arms remain *en avant* or open outward toward the audience. Later, a one-quarter turn can be made on each *relevé,* then half turns can follow.

Preparation for *pirouette en dehors* from fifth position (as seen from the front)

Center floor exercises for *pirouettes en dedans* usually are taken from fourth position with a bend or *fondu* on the forward leg only. For instance, *fondu* on the right leg, keeping the left leg straight and sole of the foot on the floor. The right arm is *en avant* and the left arm is in second position. Swing the left leg *à la seconde* at forty-five degrees as the right arm opens to second position. *Relevé* on the right foot, bringing the left foot just below the knee of the supporting leg and bringing both arms *en avant.* After the balance, the feet can lower to fifth position *demi-plié* as the arms remain *en avant* or open outward. The exercise usually begins toward a downstage corner, and the *relevé* (later the *pirouette* itself) finishes to the other downstage corner.

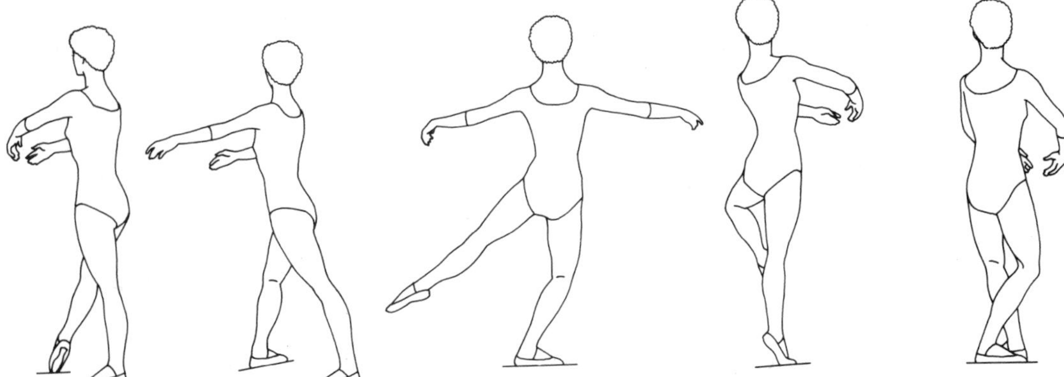

Preparation for *pirouette en dedans*
(as seen from the back)

Suggestions: Students frequently anoint the *pirouette* as the sovereign of their technical realm, approaching it with awe, honoring it with more practice than any other step, and eagerly trying every hint overheard that might ensure successful turning. There is no denying that ballet dancers must have proficiency in turning, and those who spin easily have a definite advantage over those who do not. Today's performer must be prepared to turn in every pose in the book—plus others yet untried by contemporary choreographers. But no matter how many turns are taken, they must begin cleanly and end clearly. An audience will remember the hops and staggers of a poor finish far more vividly than the number of revolutions of the *pirouettes.* Therefore, students are advised to practice the preparatory exercises diligently, taking care to keep the knees, hips, and shoulders in proper alignment at all times. Later, when a full turn is made, the closing of the arms aids in the force needed for the turn. Perhaps more important, however, will be the firm *relevé* on the supporting foot and the snap of the head in spotting.

ADAGE (ah-DAHZH), *ADAGIO*

Always an important feature of center work, the *adage* is a series of movements combining *port de bras*, exercises from *barre* work (such as *pliés*, *relevés*, *battements*), center exercises (such as *développés* to any of the positions of the body), the line poses of *arabesque* and *attitude*, and turns (usually not traveling but in place). These movements are done slowly and as though without effort, reflecting the Italian term *adagio* ("at ease" or "leisure"). The dancer must perform with coordination of the arms, legs, and head, and with a flow of movement from one pose to another. Although the *adage* must look leisurely, it is a severe test of a dancer's balance, control, and strength. It can also be a test of memory.

Learn to observe and listen carefully as the *adage* is explained. As the movements are demonstrated, try to memorize them quickly or imitate them, using minimal physical effort so that the muscles do not tire (this is called "marking" an exercise). Next will come the chance to perform the movements as completely as possible, or "full out." If the class is divided into groups, observe carefully as other groups work and learn from the corrections given them.

NOTES

1. Agrippina Vaganova, *Basic Principles of Classical Ballet* (Leningrad, 1934), trans. Anatole Chujoy (New York: Dover, 1969), 44.
2. *Ibid.*
3. Carlo Blasis, *Code of Terpsichore* (London, 1828). Republished by Dance Horizons (New York, n.d.), 74.
4. *Ibid.*
5. Erik Bruhn and Lillian Moore, *Bournonville and Ballet Technique* (London: Adam and Charles Black, 1961), 42.

CHAPTER 5
BALLET TECHNIQUE: *ALLEGRO*

The lesson thus far has been a necessary prelude to the final, perhaps most important part—the *allegro* (ah-LEH-gro). Taken from the musical term, *allegro* in ballet means the brisk, often rapid, action steps that include jumps and the connecting, auxiliary movements. These lively steps have been called the "heart and soul of ballet," with their particular quality of elevation being its "crowning glory." The performance of *allegro* is a true test of a dancer's skill, unmistakably revealed in the classical variations (solo dances in a ballet that correspond to the arias of opera).

How a dancer travels across the floor or into the air is the subject of the following pages. But first, it may be helpful to think of ballet *allegro* in very general terms.

FIVE FUNDAMENTAL MOVEMENTS OF ELEVATION

A dancer may spring

1. from both feet to both feet (the basis of *temps levé sauté*)
2. from both feet to one foot (the basis of *sissonne*)
3. from one foot to both feet (the basis of *assemblé*)
4. (or leap) from one foot to the other foot (the basis of *jeté*)
5. (or hop) on one foot (the basis of *temps levé*)

These basic movements are easiest to understand when they are done without extreme turnout of the legs. Although this procedure may sound unorthodox, it is meant only as an introduction and should lead quickly into the study of the specific steps (*pas*) of *allegro* as done from traditional ballet positions.

All jumps, leaps, and hops—whether from parallel or turned-out positions—require a bend of the knees (*plié*) for the push-off into the air and another *plié* after the jump to cushion the landing. In ballet, the landing *plié* from the first jump becomes the preparation for the next jump, thus linking the jumps together rather like the bounces of a ball. The knees and insteps of the feet act as springs; the jumps appear light and bouncy as though done from a springboard. This bouncy quality, known as *ballon* (bah-LOH*n*), gives the dancer the appearance of being airborne rather than earthbound. Indeed, in steps of very high elevation, the dancer seems to be suspended momentarily in flight. Good *ballon* often takes years to achieve, but some of the following exercises can give even the beginning student a sense of rebound from the floor. They are primarily offered, however, to introduce the five fundamental movements of elevation.

Exercises

(1) *Springs from both feet to both feet:* With the legs parallel (or with a very slight turnout), take very small jumps in place. The feet need not point fully, but the landing from each jump must be very soft, going through the toes, to the balls of the feet, to the heels as the knees bend directly over the feet. This landing is fundamental to all the jumps that follow.

(2) and (3) *Springs from both feet to one foot and from one foot to both feet:* With legs parallel (or with a very slight turnout), bend the knees and push off from two feet, landing on one foot; spring from that foot onto both. Do a series of these movements traveling across the room, forward or backward, as well as in place. (Most *allegro* steps can be done in many different directions.)

(4) *Leaps from one foot to the other foot:* Take a slow run or lope across the room. Notice that the landing of the foot is from toe to heel, not heel to toe. This is true of all landings in *allegro.* Try to lope higher, covering less space forward but more space vertically.

(5) *Hops on one foot:* These can be done in the same way as exercise 1 but on one foot, for a series of small hops, before changing to the other foot. They also can be done as a step-hop (a skip) across the floor, either forward or backward, with the arms swinging naturally. Try for higher elevation, with the knees of the bent leg lifted high in front and the other leg straight, the toes of both feet fully pointed in the air.

Combining these basic movements can quickly give a beginning student an introduction to *allegro* combinations, which later will form much of the work in the center. A sample combination of basic movements might be: three leaps forward (on the right, on the left, on the right), hop on the right, spring to both feet, spring to one foot, spring to both feet, spring to one foot. The combination should take eight counts and it could be repeated across the floor. In an as yet unrefined way the student is doing essentially: *jéte, jéte, jéte, temps levé, assemblé, sissonne, assemblé, sissonne.*

One hopes the student also is sensing some of the quality of *ballon* and the pleasure of moving across the floor to a musical beat and along with other people.

JUMPS

The first steps of elevation to be learned are jumps, which begin from and end on both feet—*temps levé sauté, soubresaut, changement de pieds,* and *échappé sauté.* These, and most other *allegro* steps, are best learned at the *barre* before they are attempted in the center floor. In many cases there are preliminary exercises that can precede the performance of the actual step—a kind of evolution helpful to the final understanding. The following general points should be kept in mind when performing these four jumps:

The preparatory movement must be a good *demi-plié*—knees bent directly over the feet and as deeply as the Achilles tendons will allow; the feet firmly on the ground at the big toes, little toes, and heels; the hips, ribs, shoulders, and head poised in perfect alignment. From the *demi-plié* there is a strong push-off from the floor—the thigh muscles contract, and the knees straighten as the feet leave the floor by a firm push through the insteps and toes. In the air the body is in alignment, the feet fully arched. The landing from the jump must be smooth; do not anticipate the floor by relaxing the points of the feet until the toes just touch the ground, then roll down through the balls and soles of the feet to the heels, allowing the knees to bend into the *demi-plié.* When the jumps first are attempted, the arms usually are carried low—in first position or *demi-seconde,* sometimes in second position. In most instances, the timing of the jump requires that the dancer be in the air on count *and,* and land on count *1.*

All *allegro* steps that follow are illustrated as seen *from the back.* The illustrated sequences read from left to right.

TEMPS LEVÉ SAUTÉ (tah*n* leh-vay soh-TAY)

Definition: Literally, the term means "raised jumped movement." The movement is simply a spring from both feet ending in the same position.

Description: This jump is learned in first position, later in second. The elements of the step are *demi-plié* in first position (or second); push directly upward into the air; land in *demi-plié* as in the starting position.

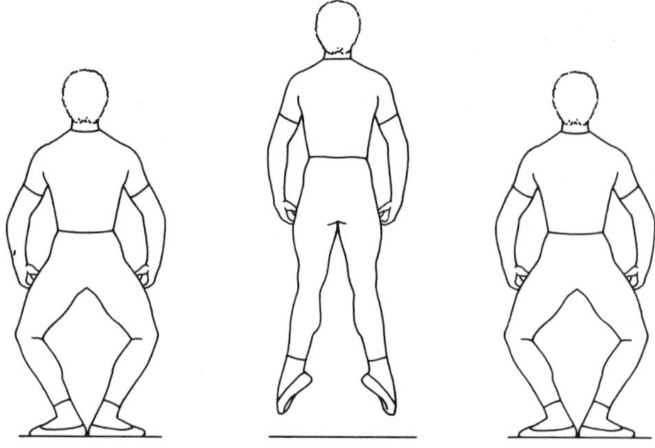

Temps levé sauté in first position

Preparatory Exercise
Relevés finishing in *demi-plié* (see page 66) done in first and second positions are basic to the understanding of *temps levés sautés* in those positions.

Other Forms: The exercise and the jump may be done in all positions of the feet.

SOUBRESAUT (soo-bruh-SOH)

Definition: This step is aptly named: *soubre* ("sudden") *saut* ("jump or jumping"). It is like a *temps levé sauté* performed in fifth position.

Description: From *demi-plié* in fifth position, push directly upward into the air with the feet tightly crossed so that no space shows between the legs. Land in *demi-plié* as in the starting position (the foot that began in front also finishes there).

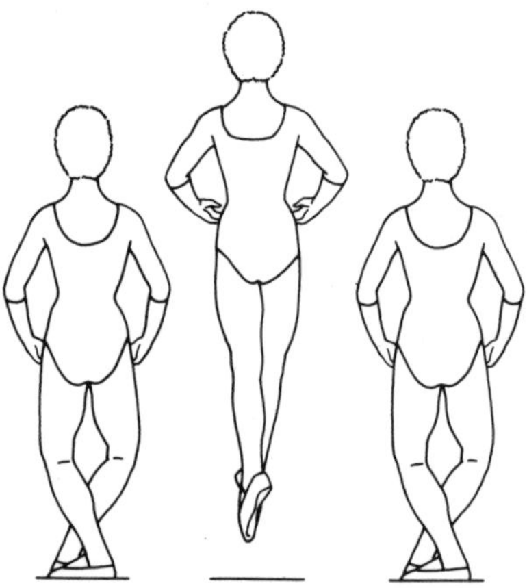

Soubresaut

Preparatory Exercise
Springing *relevés* done from fifth position (*soussus*) can introduce the tightly crossed position of the feet on the *demi-pointes.* In *soubresaut* the position is the same, except that in the air the toes can be pointed.

Other Forms: Although the simplest *soubresaut* is done in place, the step also can be done traveling forward, backward, or sideward. An advanced version is done traveling forward with the body arched and the legs thrown slightly to the back. It is known as *temps de poisson* ("fish movement").

CHANGEMENT DE PIEDS (shahnzh-mahn duh pee-AY)

Definition: Meaning "change of feet," this term usually is shortened to *changement.* It is a spring from fifth position to fifth position, landing with the foot that was in front now in back.

Description: From fifth position, right foot front, *demi-plié* and push into the air, opening the legs slightly to first position (some schools prefer less opening). Land in fifth position *demi-plié* with the left foot front (taking care that the feet do not overcross the fifth position at the finish of the *changement*).

Other Forms: *Petits changements* are sometimes done with the toes barely leaving the floor in the jump, the action happening more from the arches and ankles than from the knees and thighs. *Grands changements* are very high jumps done either with the knees sharply bent, the toes touching in the air, or with the knees straight and the legs thrown wide apart (*écarté*). Usually these versions are not attempted at the beginning level of technique.

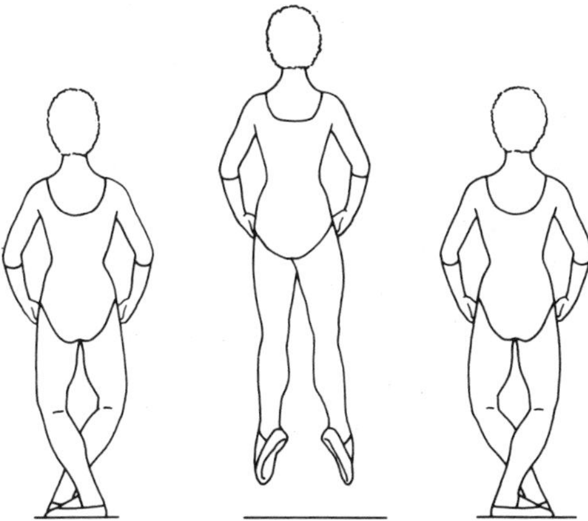

Changement de pieds

ÉCHAPPÉ SAUTÉ (ay-shah-PAY soh-TAY)

Definition: In this jump, the feet escape from a closed position to an open one, thus reflecting the meaning of the term—"escaped movement jumped."

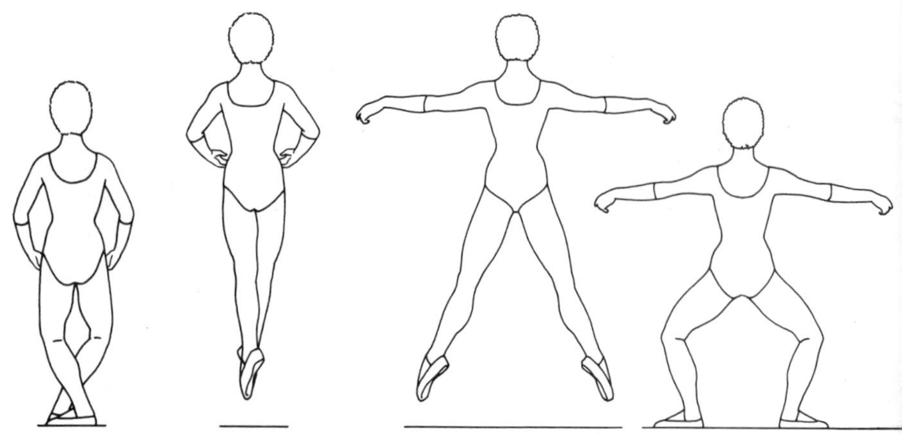

Grand échappé sauté à la seconde

Description: In *petit échappé sauté,* the jumps are not high; the legs open directly to the side before landing in second position. The return to fifth position is by another small jump. The *grand échappé sauté* requires more skill: Spring up into the air as in *soubresaut,* the feet well crossed. Open the legs to second position in the air. Land in a strong second position *demi-plié* (taking care not to pull the legs into too small a second). Spring into second position in the air. Bring the feet together in fifth position while in the air. Land in fifth position *demi-plié.*

Other Forms: The *échappé sauté* also can be done to fourth position and later with a finish on one foot instead of the return to fifth position. At a still more advanced level, the *grand échappé sauté* can be embellished with beats or a turn in the air before the legs open to second position and before they close back into fifth position.

MORE COMPLEX JUMPS

The following *allegro* steps, although considered elementary, require more coordination and considerable strength. They have many forms from simple to complex, and thus they are practiced in every level of ballet class, from beginner to professional. Before discussing the basic forms of these steps, it is wise to review some terms that will be used in describing them. Here the "working" foot refers to the foot that is the first to rise, open, or otherwise leave the original position:

Dessus (duh-SUI): The working foot passes over the supporting foot.
Dessous (duh-SOO): The working foot passes under the supporting foot.
Devant (duh-VAH*n*): The working foot begins from and ends in the front.

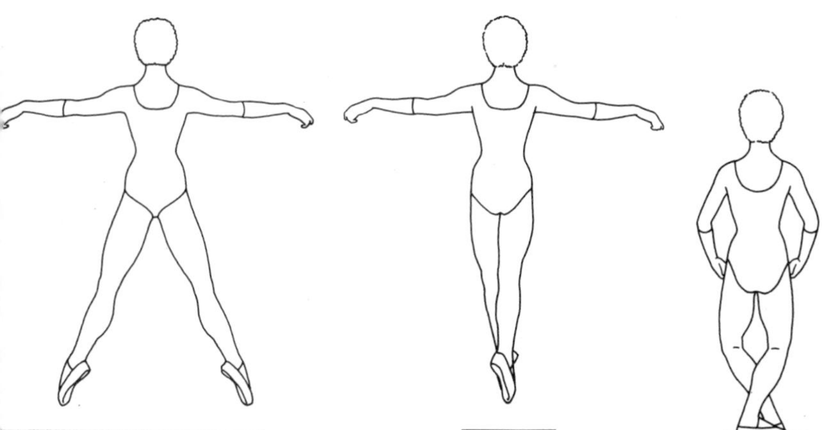

Derrière (deh-reeAIR): The working foot begins from and ends in the back.
En avant (ah-na-VAH*n*): The step is executed forward, toward the audience.
En arrière (ah-na-reeAIR): The step is executed backward, away from the audience.

ASSEMBLÉ (ah-sah*n*-BLAY)

Definition: This is a spring off of one foot onto both feet. The term means "assembled" and refers to the bringing together of the feet at the height of the jump so that the landing can be made on both feet simultaneously.

Description: *Assemblé dessus:* From fifth position, right foot back, brush the right foot to the side as the supporting knee bends deeply; without pause continue the *dégagé* movement until the right foot is off the floor. Push strongly from the floor with the supporting leg, pointing the foot in the air. Bring the legs together in the air, the right foot in front of the left, both feet still pointed. Alight simultaneously on both feet in a *demi-plié* with the right foot front in fifth position.

The following variations are described only briefly, the essential action of the legs remaining the same as in the *assemblé dessus.*

Assemblé dessous: The front foot brushes to the side and closes in back.
Assemblé devant: The front foot brushes to the side and returns to the front.
Assemblé derrière: The back foot brushes to the side and returns to the back.
Assemblé en avant: The front foot brushes forward and returns to the front.
Assemblé en arrière: The back foot brushes backward and returns to the back.

The *assemblés en avant* and *en arrière* require somewhat greater control, especially of the spine, and therefore are the last of this series to be learned.

Preparatory Exercise
As a preparation for *assemblé dessus*, from fifth position, right foot back, *dégagé* to the side with the back foot as the supporting knee bends. *Relevé* high on the supporting foot, close the right foot front and *demi-plié* on both feet in fifth position. From that same *demi-plié*, begin the exercise with the left foot brushing to the side, and so forth. Reverse the entire action as a preparation for *assemblé dessous.* The other *assemblés* can benefit from similar exercises, learned at the *barre.* As center exercises they are particularly challenging.

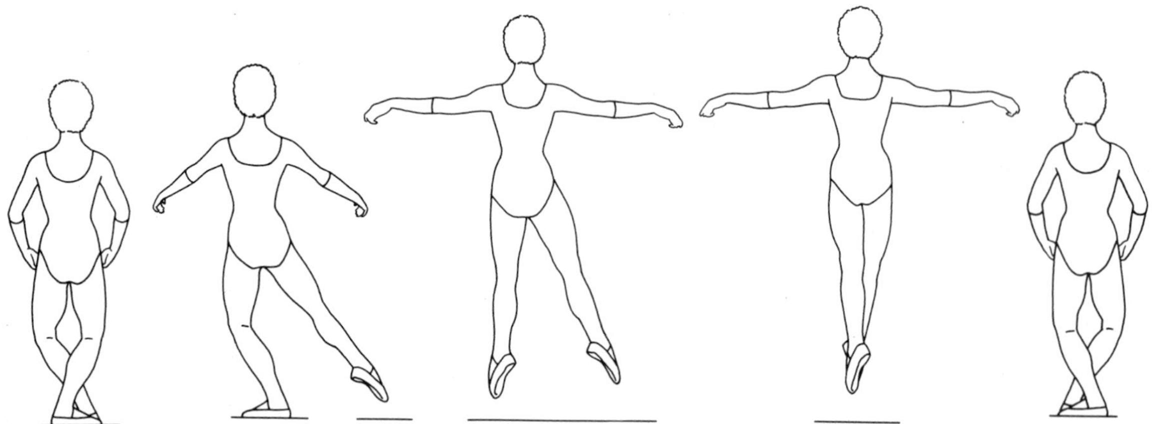

Assemblé dessus

Other Forms: Although all of the *assemblés* described here are done in place (with only small progressions forward or backward because of the closing position of the feet), they also can be done traveling from one spot to another, known as *assemblé porté* ("carried"). When an *assemblé* is started from one foot, with the leg already in some position in the air, it is called *assemblé coupé* ("cut"). Advanced forms are the *assemblé en tournant,* which is performed with a turn in the air, and the *assemblé battu,* in which the legs beat before they are assembled for the close.

SISSONNE (see-SON)

Definition: The *sissonne* is basically a spring off of both feet onto one foot and as such represents the second half of a dance step called *pas de sissonne* in eighteenth-century texts. Scholars have speculated that the step, no doubt of earlier origin, was named for its inventor.

Description: The most elementary form is *sissonne simple* (SA*n*-pluh) and is performed like a *soubresaut* but with a finish on one foot in *fondu*, with the other foot pointed just above the supporting ankle, either front (*devant*) or back (*derrière*). In other forms the qualifying term *ouverte* (oo-VAIRT), meaning "open," is added if the raised foot remains in the air, and the term *fermée* (fair-MAY), or "closed," is added if the raised foot closes quickly after the other foot into fifth position *demi-plié*.

The following two *sissonnes* are done traveling to the side (*de côté*) with a change of feet. They are not high jumps, but are done quickly and with the legs raised only to half-height (*á la demi-hauteur*):

Sissonne fermée dessus: From fifth position *demi-plié*, spring into the air, travel sideward toward the front foot as the back foot opens to second position. Land on the front foot in *fondu;* quickly slide the other foot to fifth position front.

Sissonne fermée dessus

Sissonne fermée dessous: Perform as above but travel in the direction of the back foot and finish with the other foot in back.

Other Forms: *Sissonnes* can be done traveling forward or backward in various positions of the body, and with or without a change of feet. They may be done turning and with beats.

TEMPS LEVÉ (tah*n* luh-VAY)

Definition: *Temps levé*, meaning "movement raised," is a hop on one foot with the other foot raised to any given position.

Description: Usually in beginning classes, the raised foot is fully arched, toes pointed downward, and placed just above the ankle, either in front (*sur le cou-de-pied devant*) or in back (*sur le cou-de-pied derrière*). The hop necessitates a strong *fondu* on the supporting leg, then a spring from the floor that is high enough for the leg to straighten completely, foot arched and toes pointed. The return to the ground is to that same leg, lowering in *fondu.*

Preparatory Exercises
Fondus and *relevés*, with the raised foot *sur le cou-de-pied devant* or *derrière*, can be incorporated in *barre* exercises to prepare for *temps levé.* They first should be practiced slowly, then with gradually increased speed, but always in moderation. Both this exercise and the *allegro* step are strenuous.

Other Forms: *Temps levé en arabesque* and *en attitude* are more advanced versions of the basic movement. In the Cecchetti method, *temps levé* also can refer to a spring from fifth position with the other foot raised to a *cou-de-pied* position (*sissonne simple*, in other methods).

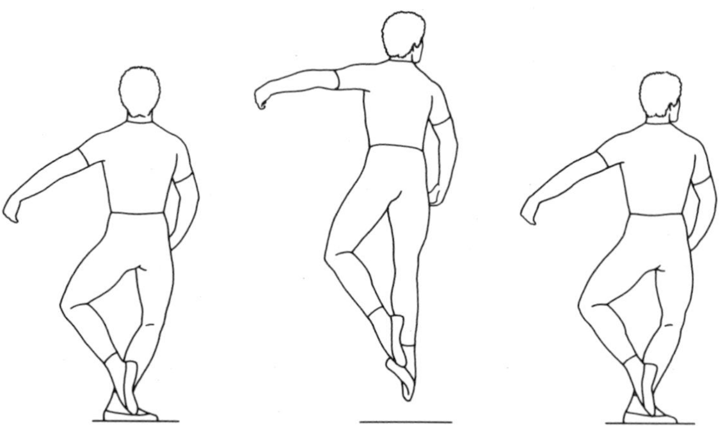

Temps levé sur le cou-de-pied derrière

JETÉ (zhuh-TAY)

Definition: *Jeté* means "thrown." It is a spring from one foot to the other, done with a strong brush or "throw" of the leg into the air.

Description: The most basic *jetés* are the following two:

Jeté dessus: From fifth position, right foot back, *demi-plié* and brush the back foot into the air (as in *battement dégagé* to the side); then spring upward from the supporting foot so that for a moment both legs are straight and both feet are pointed in the air. Land in *fondu* on the right foot just in front of the spot vacated by the supporting foot, which now points just above and in back of the right ankle. To continue in a series, brush the back (left) foot into the air from its pointed position at the ankle.

Jeté dessous: Perform as above, but brush the front foot to the side and finish the step with it in back, the other foot pointed just above and in front of the ankle.

The direction of movement for *jetés dessus* and *dessous* is up; they are thrown straight into the air and do not travel from side to side.

Preparatory Exercise
This is a preparation for *jeté dessus.* From fifth position, right foot back, *dégagé* the back foot to the side while bending the supporting knee, *relevé* on the supporting foot, bring the right foot momentarily to fifth position front, and immediately lower onto it in *fondu.* When the transfer of weight is made, the left foot arches just above and behind the right ankle. Continue in the same manner, brushing the left foot to the side from its pointed position (now more like the action of a *battement frappé*). Reverse the entire action as a preparation for *jetés dessous.*

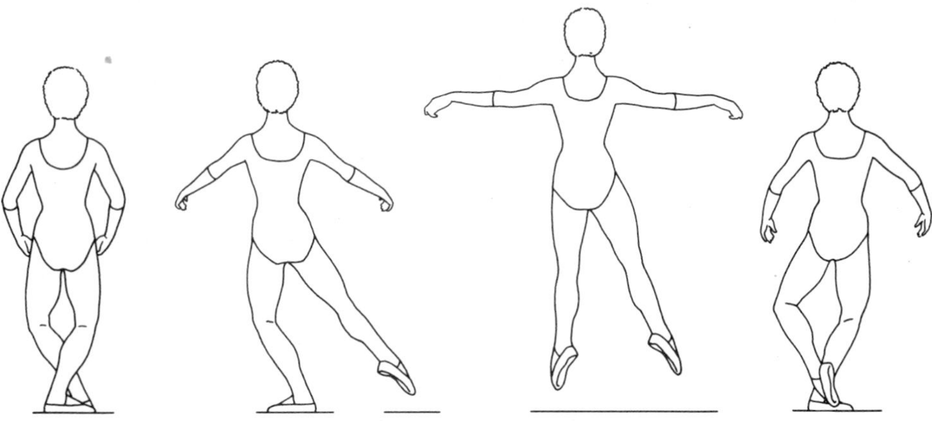

Jeté dessus

Other Forms: *Jetés* may be very small or very large, and may be performed with beats, turns, or without a brush. Probably no *allegro* step is as much fun to do as the *grand jeté en avant,* a big leap forward in which one leg is thrown into the air as for *grand battement* to the front as the other leg pushes strongly from the floor; the body tries to remain momentarily in the air in a definite pose of *attitude* or *arabesque* and then alights in that same pose. The *grand jeté* (as it is commonly called) is often preceded by a *pas couru* ("running step") to give it the necessary push-off. Another step, frequently called *tour jeté*, is one in which the body makes a sharp 180-degree turn in the air as the legs pass close to each other in a scissorslike motion. These, and other forms of *jeté*, are not described in detail here because they are seldom part of beginning classes.

PAS DE CHAT (pah duh SHAH)

Definition: The term means "step of the cat" and implies the step's quick, catlike springing movement from one foot to the other.

Description: There are several styles of this step, but the beginning student usually learns the following versions:

Petit pas de chat: From fifth position, right foot back, *demi-plié* and raise the back foot, arched, to the ankle of the left foot; immediately spring upward and to the side, raising the left foot to the same height as the first foot; land in *fondu* on the first foot and quickly follow with the other foot closing to fifth position front in *demi-plié.*

Petit pas de chat

Grand pas de chat: Perform exactly as above, but raise the foot to the height of the knee (*retiré* position) and spring higher into the air.

CONNECTING MOVEMENTS

Jumps are not always done one right after another. Instead, they often are linked together by connecting steps. Because they are done close to the ground, these steps give contrast to the high jump that will follow and serve as a preparation for and introduction to the more exciting step. The connecting steps have another purpose—to carry the dancer from one spot to another. When done in a series and with *épaulement,* these relatively small and simple movements have a charm of their own.

GLISSADE (glee-SAHD)

Definition: Meaning "to glide," *glissade* is done close to the ground, with a brush of one foot along the floor, a shift of weight to that foot, and a slide into fifth position by the other foot.

Description: The following *glissades* travel to the side, beginning and ending with the same foot in front. The feet must not be lifted high off the floor, even though at one moment both legs are straight and both feet are fully pointed. The entire action of the step is timed *and 1,* with the close to fifth position on count *1.*

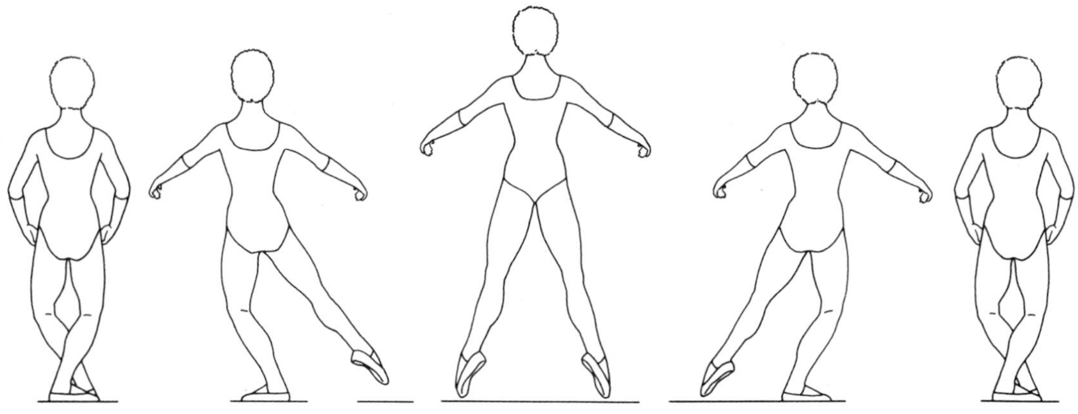

Glissade derrière

Glissade derrière: From fifth position, right foot back, *demi-plié* and extend the back foot along the floor to the side, finishing with the foot fully arched and toes pointed a few inches off the floor, the left leg remaining in *fondu.* With a slight spring, shift the weight to the right leg in *fondu,* extending the left leg as the left foot points just slightly off the floor. Quickly slide the left foot into fifth position front in *demi-plié.*

Glissade devant: Perform as above but begin with the front foot, which remains in front at the close.

In the following *glissades*, the basic action and timing of the legs are the same as above, but they are done with a change of feet (sometimes called *glissade changée*, especially when done in a series):

Glissade dessous: Travel to the side, beginning with the front foot, which finishes in back.

Glissade dessus: Travel to the side, beginning with the back foot, which finishes in front.

Glissades also may travel forward or backward *en face* or on the diagonals. The basic action and timing remain the same:

Glissade en arrière: Travel backward, beginning with the back foot, which finishes in back.

Glissade en avant: Travel forward, beginning with the front foot, which finishes in front.

Preparatory Exercise
To learn the *glissade,* break the step down into four slow parts: From fifth position *demi-plié,* extend one foot along the floor (count 1); shift the weight onto that foot in *fondu* (count 2); slide the other foot into fifth position *demi-plié* (count 3); hold the *demi-plié* (count 4).

COUPÉ (koo-PAY)

Definition: *Coupé* means "cut." As a step it has many forms, all involving one foot "cutting away" the other in order to replace it. Usually this occurs as a preparation for another step, but sometimes *coupés* are performed in a series from one foot to the other.

Description: *Coupés* are done *dessous* (one foot cutting under) or *dessus* (one foot cutting over) to replace the supporting foot. This may be done jumped in the air (*sauté*) or with a rise through the *demi-pointes* along the ground (*par terre*).

Coupé dessous sauté: Fondu on the right foot as the left foot arches just above and in back of the right ankle. Spring into the air just high enough to allow the right foot to arch, toes pointing downward, and land on the left foot in *fondu*, right foot arched just above and in front of the left ankle. This can be reversed for *coupé dessus,* in which case the front foot cuts over the back foot.

Coupé dessous par terre: From *pointe tendue* fourth position back, *fondu* on the supporting leg. Draw the back foot to the front foot in fifth position on the *demi-pointes. Fondu* on the back leg as the front foot extends to *pointe tendue* fourth position front. This version too can be reversed for *coupé dessus,* in which case the front foot cuts over the back foot.

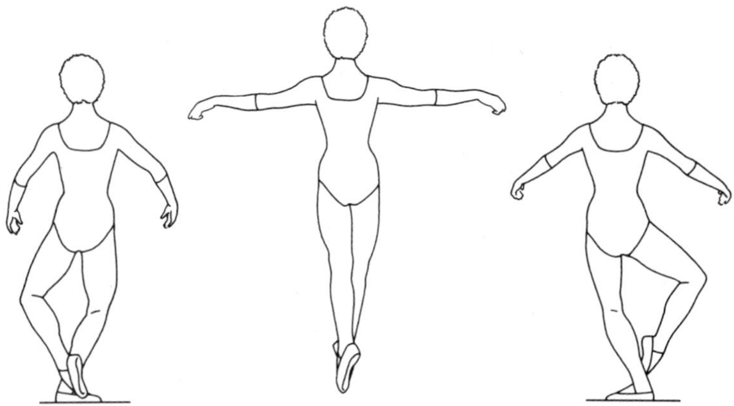

Coupé dessous sauté

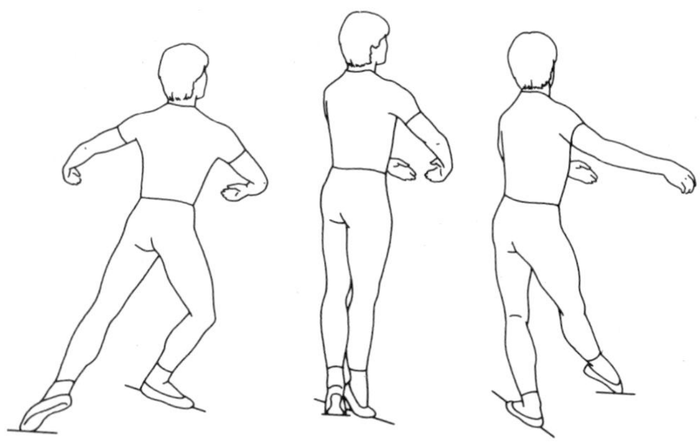

Coupé dessous par terre

PAS DE BOURRÉE (pah duh boo-RAY)

Definition: The *bourrée* was a French folk dance form, court dance form, and musical form. The *pas de bourrée*, or "*bourrée* step," had dozens of variations in early eighteenth-century dance technique. Today's ballet vocabulary contains considerably fewer, with six versions commonly appearing in elementary classes. Although the actual performance of the steps has changed, now, as then, the *pas de bourrée* involves three movements—either three shifts of weight or two shifts of weight and then a closing to position.

Description: In general, if the preparation is a *dégagé,* the *pas de bourrée* will finish in fifth position *demi-plié.* If, however, the *pas de bourrée* begins with one foot raised in front or back of the ankle, it usually will finish in a *fondu* with the other foot in the raised position. The first method is described and illustrated here.

Pas de bourrée dessous: From fifth position, left foot front or back, *demi-plié* and *dégagé* to second position with the left foot (this is a preparatory movement that occurs on count "and"). Draw the left foot to fifth position in back of the right foot as both feet rise to the *demi-pointes.* Immediately open the right foot to second position and step onto *demi-pointe.* Close the left foot front in fifth position *demi-plié.*

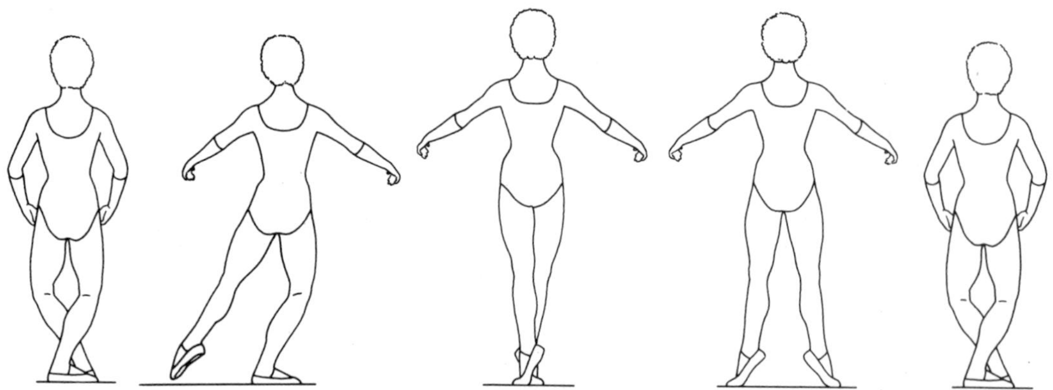

Pas de bourrée dessous

Pas de bourrée dessus: Perform as above, but after the preparatory *dégagé,* step in front, then to the side, and close the first foot in back.

Pas de bourrée derrière: Perform as above, but step in back, then to the side, and close in back.

Pas de bourrée devant: Perform as above, but step in front, then to the side, and close in front.

Pas de bourrée en arrière: From *pointe tendue* in fourth position, right foot front, bring the right foot to fifth position front stepping onto *demi-pointe,* immediately open the left foot, and take a small step backward onto *demi-pointe;* close the right foot front in *fondu* as the left foot extends to *pointe tendue* in fourth position back.

Pas de bourrée en avant: Perform as above, but begin from fourth position back, bring the foot to fifth position, step forward, and close back as the other foot extends to the front.

Both the *pas de bourrée en arrière* and *en avant* may start from fifth position with a preparatory *dégagé* to the *tendue* position, and they may finish in fifth position *demi-plié.* They are usually performed to the *effacé* or *croisé* directions.

Other Forms: *Pas de bourrée piqué* means that the feet are picked up sharply to the height of the ankle or knee on each step. In *pas de bourrée fondu,* the second step is made in *fondu* rather than to *demi-pointe.* In more advanced training, *pas de bourrée* is done *en tournant,* either *en dehors* (turning outward with a *pas de bourrée dessous*) or *en dedans* (turning inward with a *pas de bourrée dessus*). Tiny running steps traveling in any direction are called *pas de bourrée couru.* They are done with the feet tightly crossed in fifth position on the *demi-pointes* (later on full point for advanced women students), or without turnout (in parallel position).

CHASSÉ (shah-SAY)

Definition: When performed in a series, *chassés* ("chased") give the appearance of one foot chasing the other from its position. The term has also come to apply to a connecting movement made by a slide of the foot from fifth position *demi-plié* to second or fourth position.

Description: *Chassés* can travel forward, backward, or sideward. When performing them in a series, the dancer should have the appearance of skimming or sliding, not galloping, across the floor. The following version, beginning with a preparatory spring into the air (similar to a *sissonne simple* or *temps levé* from two feet to one foot) represents one of several styles of *chassé:*

Chassé en l'air en avant: Facing a downstage corner, *demi-plié* in fifth position, right foot front. Spring into the air, alight on the left foot in *fondu* with the right foot arched in front of the supporting ankle, the toes close to the ground. Immediately slide the right foot forward to fourth position, transferring the weight to the right leg in *fondu* as the left leg extends, foot pointing on, or close to, the ground. To repeat, spring forward into the air, immediately closing the left leg behind the right, alight in *fondu* on the left foot, and continue as above. The same basic action applies to *chassés à la seconde* (after the preparatory spring, slide the front foot to second position and travel sideward) and to the more difficult *chassés en arrière* (after the preparatory spring, land on the front foot and slide the back foot to fourth position and travel backward).

Chassé en l'air en avant

Preparatory Exercise
Before attempting *chassés en l'air,* it is helpful to practice the movements as described above, but with *relevés* instead of springs into the air.

Other Forms: More advanced versions include *chassé passé* (with a change of feet, passing the foot through first to fourth position) and *chassé en tournant* (performed with a turn in the air).

ADDITIONAL *ALLEGRO* STEPS

Each of the following steps contains three transfers of weight, usually each shift of weight occurring on each beat of a 3/4 measure of music, such as a waltz rhythm. Related versions of these steps are found in some folk dances.

BALANCÉ (bah-lah*n*-SAY)

Definition: The verb *balancer* can mean "to swing or rock to and fro." The step *balancé* has shifts of weight from one foot to the other and may involve movement from side to side or forward and backward.

Description: *Balancé* is a step of many moods: sometimes it is bouncy and performed with a light *jeté;* other times it is romantic and performed with a low glide along the floor. In all *balancés* the legs must remain very turned out, and the lowering to *fondu* must be done softly. The following version is done *de côté* ("to the side") and usually begins with the back foot:

Balancé de côté: From fifth position, right foot back, *demi-plié* and extend the right foot to the side; transfer the weight onto the right foot in *fondu.* Bring the left foot directly behind the right foot and shift the weight onto the left *demi-pointe*, raising the right foot just off the ground. *Fondu* in place on the right foot, arching the left foot behind the right ankle. The *balancé* can now be repeated to the left side.

Balancé de côté

Other Forms: *Balancés* may be performed *en avant* or *en arrière* ("forward" or "backward") in any of the positions of the body. They may be done *en tournant*, completing one half-turn on each *balancé*.

PAS DE BASQUE (pah duh BAHSK)

Definition: The "Basque step," commonly found in folk dances of almost every country, takes its name from the Basques, a people of the Pyrenees region of southern France and northern Spain. In its simplest form it is not unlike the *balancé*, except that after the first step to the side, the movement is always forward or backward.

Description: The *pas de basque* frequently begins facing one downstage corner and finishes to the other. It has many forms: it may be jumped or glided, large or small, or it may turn. A variety of *port de bras* can be used in the following versions:

Pas de basque sauté en avant: From fifth position, right foot front, *demi-plié* and, with the right foot, execute a *demi-rond de jambe en dehors* (that is, extend the foot forward and then to the side) slightly above the floor. Spring to the side onto the right foot, bringing the left foot arched in front of the right ankle (or just below the right knee). Step or *piqué* forward onto the left foot, bringing the right foot arched behind the left ankle (or just behind the left knee). *Coupé dessous* with the right foot, arching the left foot in front of the supporting ankle. The *pas de basque* now can be repeated to the left side. All movements can be reversed to perform the *pas de basque sauté en arrière.*

Pas de basque sauté en avant

Pas de basque glissé en avant: From fifth position, right foot front, *demi-plié* and, with the right foot, execute a *demi-rond de jambe en dehors à terre.* Shift the weight onto the right foot in *fondu,* extending the left foot *pointe*

Pas de basque glissé en avant

tendue à la seconde. Slide the left foot through first position *demi-plié* (some styles like it also to slide into fifth position) and forward into fourth position, remaining in *demi-plié.* Shift the weight onto the left foot as both legs straighten. Slide the right foot into fifth position behind in *demi-plié.* The *pas de basque* can now be repeated to the left side, or all movements reversed for *pas de basque glissé en arrière.*

ALLEGRO COMBINATIONS

When several steps are joined together to be performed to a musical phrase, it is called a combination or *enchaînement* (ah*n*-shain-MAH*n*), literally, a "linking." *Allegro* combinations are the student's first taste of what it may be to dance—to perform one step after another, in time to music, with a definite beginning, middle, and ending of a dance and musical phrase. Some examples of *enchaînements* are suggested here.

PETIT ALLEGRO COMBINATIONS

These combinations may be performed to a 2/4 or 4/4 rhythm and repeated four times. Combinations that progress forward should then be reversed so that they progress backward.

1. *Changement, changement, petit échappé sauté* to second position and back to fifth position with a change of feet.
2. *Glissade derrière, assemblé dessus, assemblé dessous, changement.*
3. *Jeté dessus, jeté dessus, pas de bourrée dessous* (finishing on one foot), *temps levé* on that foot.

GRAND ALLEGRO COMBINATIONS

These larger combinations may be performed in 3/4 or 6/8 rhythm and repeated two or four times. They require more strength than the *petit* combinations.

1. *Chassé en l'air en avant* three times, finishing the last *chassé* in *pas de bourrée dessous, glissade derrière, assemblé dessus, soussus, changement.*
2. *Grand échappé sauté* to second position and back to fifth position without a change of feet, repeat the *échappé* but this time change the feet, *sissonne ouverte en avant* raising the back leg to a low *attitude, jeté dessus en attitude, jeté dessus en attitude, assemblé coupé derrière.*
3. *Balancé de côté, balancé de côté,* three *chaînés tours,* step into first *arabesque fondue,* hold, *pas de bourrée dessous, pas de chat.*

A combination, indeed any single step, requires coordinated arm and head movements if it is to be more than mere physical drill. Beginners learn the basic small jumps with the arms carried simply *en bas,* or in first position, the head straight. At that stage of learning, it is important to train the upper body, head, and arms not to react to the movement of the legs; flapping arms, jiggling shoulders, and a seesaw spine are to be avoided from the very beginning. But in steps such as *glissade* or *assemblé,* where the legs open out from the body, the beginner should open the arms also, usually to *demi-seconde.* Later, steps of high elevation such as *grand échappé sauté,* large *assemblés,* or *sissonnes* benefit from arms (*not* shoulders) that rise to higher positions as the height of the jump is reached. Changes of body direction also add interest to *allegro* work. For instance, in the third *petit allegro* combination suggested above, the two *jetés* can be done *en face* but with *épaulement* (head and shoulders in alignment with the working leg) and the arms *en bas.* The *pas de bourrée* can finish with the body on the diagonal, the arms in *croisé devant* and the head inclined toward the audience, where they remain for the *temps levé.* Such coordination requires great skill and is the result of many classes, great patience, and determination to try and try and try, and then try once again.

BEATS

Beginners' classes do not deal with beats, but the curiosity and misunderstanding beginning students often have about them prompt this brief discussion.

Once basic *allegro* steps are mastered, many of them are embellished, and some are performed exclusively with beats. These include such small steps as the *entrechats* ("braidings or interweavings")–jumps with rapid crossings of the legs in the air. The beats are made as the calves of the legs open out and close in, crossing in front and behind each other. Since both legs are active in the movement, they are both counted; for example, in an *entrechat quatre,* because each leg makes two crossings, the step counts as four (*quatre*) beats. A few dancers (male) have managed five crossings—an *entrechat dix*. An uneven number, as in *entrechat trois* (three), usually indicates a finish on one foot or in an open position (second or fourth).

Beaten steps requiring higher elevation include the *cabrioles* ("capers"), in which one leg is thrown into the air followed by the underneath leg, which beats against it, sending the first leg even higher into the air.

The broad term for these and all other steps with beats is *batterie* (bat-REE). Since the *batterie* is best performed when the legs are very warm, it is most commonly given at the end of class.

RÉVÉRENCE (ray-vay-RAH*n*S)

The ballet class may end with a last flourish of jumps, or it may conclude with slow *pliés, relevés, grands battements*, or *port de bras* to allow the students to wind down after working vigorously for an hour or more. In either case, the final movement of class is often the *révérence*, a bow or curtsey taken by teacher and class in appreciation of their mutual effort.

A *révérence* may range in form from simple to elaborate. For a woman it is often a step to the side as the arms open to second position; the other foot is then brought behind the supporting foot, and the knees bend as the body leans slightly forward from the hips. A man may simply step forward, bringing the other foot close with the knee relaxed, arms remaining at the side as the head bows forward.

The *révérence* taken in class is not unlike the one a performer may take in acknowledgment of applause. Indeed, there is even applause after the class *réverénce*, whereby the students formally thank the instructor for the lesson.

POSTSCRIPT

These, then, are some of the fundamentals of ballet technique—to be learned by the beginner and to be practiced daily by the aspiring dancer. Words and drawings can help analyze the mechanics of movements, but they are meager tools when it comes to communicating the *sensation* of a movement, the way it *feels*. Some people believe that mental images can help students toward a deeper sensation and understanding. For instance, a *plié* could be imagined as starting, not just from the thighs, but very high in the center of the torso, so that the action is sensed as a slow opening of the body, right down the middle, into two equal halves. (This "halving" is easier to sense when a student stands between two *barres* or chairs, one hand holding onto each.) As another example, when a leg is lifted, as in *grand battement* to the front, one could imagine that the force for the *battement* comes from deep within the body down the back of the leg, thus throwing the leg lightly into the air. Or, the *grand battement* could be sensed as though a string were pulled tightly and then released slowly to allow the leg to descend smoothly.

The visual excitement of watching a truly fine dancer comes, ultimately, from the dancer's look of oneness with the movement. Steps do not seem pasted on but as though they grew outward from the very core of the dancer. Tamara Karsavina wisely advises students:

> Do not discard your "feel" of the movement as you do your practice tunic at the end of the class. Take it with you on the bus or the train; there is no extra fare for it. Remember that the mechanism of the dance becomes artistry only when it is inspired by feeling and that feeling perpetuated in your mind will pass into your movements.[1]

NOTE

1. Tamara Karsavina, *Classical Ballet: The Flow of Movement* (London: Adam & Charles Black, 1962), 15.

CHAPTER 6
THE BALLET BODY

Probably no one spends more time in front of full-length mirrors than the dancer; probably few people other than doctors and hypochondriacs spend as much time discussing bodies. This preoccupation is not surprising, because for the art of dance, unlike the other arts, the human body is the essential element.

THE IDEAL PHYSIQUE

The studio mirror reveals many shapes and sizes, seldom a perfect ballet image. Nevertheless, the female student longs to see the ideal reflection: a head neither too large nor too small, well-poised on a slim neck; shoulders of some width but with a slope gently downward; small bust, waist, and buttocks; a back that is straight but not rigid; well-formed arms hanging relaxed from the shoulders; delicate hands; slim, straight legs with smooth lines both in back and in front; a compact foot that arches easily—all this totaling a slim silhouette of ballet perfection. The ideal male physique is not as specific, although it is generally considered to be strong and well muscled without excess weight or bulk, the shoulders wider than the waist and hips, and minimal height now probably about five feet, eight inches.

Rarely does a dancer have an ideal ballet body; indeed some dancers have succeeded as fine performers in spite of structural characteristics that would seem to preclude a ballet career. And ballet fashions change. The current fad is for bodies considerably thinner and taller than those of earlier eras. Pictures of those plump ballerinas and short, stocky *danseurs* look quaintly amusing to the streamlined eyes of today's dancers (although to most ballet parents they look a great deal healthier than the skinny dancers of the present).

Even though fashionable body aesthetics do change, the ideal of balanced proportions for a dancer's body does not. Celia Sparger, an authority on ballet physique, observes:

> The body which is well proportioned will weather the stresses and strains of the exacting work required of it with greater ease than one in which there is some disparity in the relative length, for instance, of limbs to torso, of width to length of the body, or the relative size of shoulders to hips and so on. . . . Moreover, in the well-formed, well-proportioned physique there is less likelihood of muscles thickening in unwanted places, and less proneness to the minor and sometimes major mishaps caused by the effort to overcome obstacles which are inherent in the build of the body.[1]

She suggests using the characteristic proportions of classical Greece as a guide: the length from the top of the head to the pubic junction is equal to that from the junction to the ground, and the length from the junction to the lower border of the knee cap is equal to that from the lower border of the knee cap to the ground.

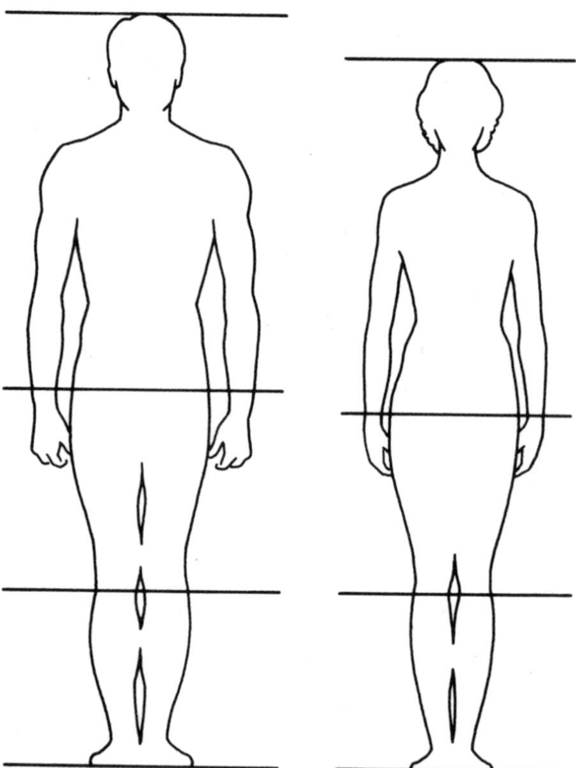

Ideally proportioned bodies

PREVENTING INJURY

Almost any form of physical activity, certainly one as demanding as ballet, raises the possibility of injury, and even a well-proportioned body will suffer from strenuous movements or stretches if inadequately warmed up. The fundamental exercises at the *barre* have as one of their important functions, then, the systematic warming up of the body. When these exercises are neglected before a rehearsal or performance, or by a latecomer to class, then injury is invited. Moreover, each *barre* exercise has its specific purpose, as was seen in Chapter 3. Incorrect or minimal performance of any of those exercises can result in aches and pains, sometimes serious injury.

The correct execution of each exercise is the dancer's fundamental safeguard against injury. To quote Sparger once more:

> Ballet has its own technique of definite and exact movements. *If these movements are performed correctly, the correct muscles will work.* If the movement is not performed correctly, wrong muscles will come into play. . . . The dancer cannot begin by trying to find out which muscles to use. The right effort will eventually ensure right muscle work.[2]

This is not to say that a dancer should be ignorant of how the body's muscles function, but it does imply the importance of slow, careful, and intelligent work guided by the informed and responsive teacher. Sparger's statement also implies the necessity of a clear understanding of a particular movement—its dynamics, direction, and shape.

Correct ballet movement includes alternate stretching and relaxation. For instance, in a *battement tendu* the foot is stretched along the floor and then returned to the closed position, where it must relax before the stretch begins again. Whenever possible the weight should be momentarily transferred to both feet in the closed position. If this brief relaxation is omitted, cramps may occur along the sides or arches of the feet; when the relaxation is systematically omitted, the muscles in the calf and thigh may cramp. Eventually those muscles will become hard and bulky, lacking the essential elasticity for ballet.

The order of exercises at the *barre* can also prevent a muscle-bound look. Exercises are done to all directions; that is *grands battements* done to the front, which contract the thigh muscles, are countered by *grands battements* to the back, which stretch those muscles. *Relevés,* which tighten the calf muscles, are followed by *demi-pliés,* which relieve that tension.

The overenthusiastic student can be cruelly rewarded by an injury to a body pushed beyond its technical scope or past its endurance point. Fatigue or inadequate eating habits can have debilitating effects on the dancer.

Improper body alignment can contribute to weaknesses that in turn may trigger injury. Knees seem to be especially vulnerable, and special care must be taken in the training of students with knock-knees or bowlegs. Hyperextended (swayback) knees sometimes call for special consideration, particularly in attempts to improve body placement and hip alignment. To do this, it is helpful for the student to work for a time at the *barre* with the legs in parallel instead of turned-out positions, the weight shifted more forward by tilting the pelvis up on the hip. *Demi-pliés*, *relevés*, and *battements* done to the front with legs parallel and with muscular control keeping the knees stable but not locked may help bring a hip into alignment and take pressure off the back of the knees. Another suggestion to help achieve correct ballet placement (often a readjustment of the placement of body weight) is for the student to stand between two *barres*, thus having a double *barre*. When the studio is not equipped with portable *barres*, chairs can be placed parallel to one another and the student can stand between them, holding onto both during the execution of various exercises.

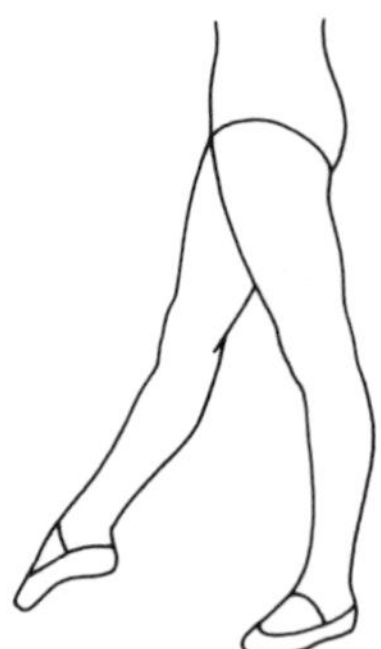

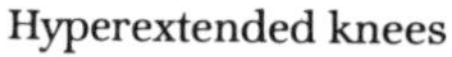

Hyperextended knees

Knees brought into better alignment

Still, in spite of careful classwork, a particular exercise may seem difficult or even impossible for an adult beginning the study of ballet, but restricted in movement range after years of postural and movement habits. For some, additional study with body therapy experts may result in changes of habitual ways of standing or moving that in turn will facilitate ballet poses and movements.[3]

COMMON INJURIES AND AILMENTS

"If it hurts, it's good for you," is not good advice; pain may well be the body's warning to cease dance activity. Following is a brief discussion of some injuries and ailments that can occur to dance students.

CRAMP

A sudden muscle cramp during class should be a vivid reminder to warm up properly and to guard against the buildup of tensions during exercises (for instance, when possible, return the weight to both feet between movements that use one leg only). A cramp can be relieved by immediate gentle stretching of the cramped muscle, accompanied by massage. Soreness may result, but if the cramp is *fully* relieved before work is resumed, there will be no serious damage.

MUSCLE SORENESS

Sore muscles, a fairly common complaint from students who are not used to practicing ballet exercises regularly, can be a kind of "sweet pain," seldom long-lasting or in any way debilitating. The best remedy is to increase circulation by working the muscle lightly again as soon as possible. Prevention of soreness, or its often-accompanying stiffness, includes, besides sufficient warming up and gentle stretching, an adequate warming down—end-of-class *battements*, *pliés*, and *ports de bras* exercises (the dancer's equivalent of a race horse's walking routine following the race).

STRAIN

Dancers often display a stoical pride in ignoring or minimizing nagging pains that should alert them to the possibility of a serious injury. One such injury, called a strain, is a tearing of muscles and tendons, usually occurring anywhere from the hips down. The common causes can be structural weakness, previous injury or severe illness, overfatigue, or incorrect execution of an exercise (sometimes the very first exercise at *barre*, the *plié*). A strain produces stiffness and pain when the injured part is used. Swelling can occur too, but it can be minimized if the following procedures are observed:

1. Immediately apply pressure to the injured part by snugly wrapping it with a wet elastic ("Ace") bandage.
2. Apply ice compresses for twenty to thirty minutes to the injury and to an area well above and below it.
3. Elevate the injured part.

Heat can be applied after all possibility of swelling is gone, usually at least twenty-four hours later. Even a minor strain or "muscle pull" must be allowed time to heal; it cannot be "worked out."

SPRAIN

A sprain is damage to ligaments of a joint, occurring most frequently in the ankle joint, but sometimes in hip or knee joints. A violent stretch or twist or fall can produce a sprain, but so also can incorrect knee-to-foot alignment during jumps or overly zealous attempts to turn out the feet beyond the range permitted by the hip joint. The injured joint will be very painful and sometimes impossible to use. To achieve a speedy recovery, swelling must be controlled as quickly as possible. Immediate treatment should include the three procedures listed above: pressure, ice, and elevation (PIE, for short), then immobilization of the joint to avoid further tearing of ligament fibers. Any such taping or bandaging should be done by, or in consultation with, a specialist. Uninformed treatment can be injurious.

DISLOCATION AND FRACTURE

The same preliminary treatment also applies to such other serious injuries as dislocations (a bone thrown out of joint) and fractures, unless the fracture is compound (broken bone sticking through the skin), fortunately a rare occurrence for dancers. In all cases of severe injury (including strains and sprains), a doctor (preferably an orthopedic physician) should be consulted without delay. Often helpful advice can be obtained from an athletic trainer on campus.

BRUISES

The most debilitating bruise for the dancer is the "stone bruise" on the ball of the foot, sometimes a result of repetitious jumping, especially on hard surfaces. Poorly executed exercises, such as *battements frappés* in which the foot is pounded against the floor during brushes outward, can contribute to a contusion or bruise. Cold compresses wrapped around the foot should be applied at once. Later, gentle stretching and application of heat may be helpful.

SHIN SPLINTS

The most common definition given of shin splints is a minor tearing of the muscle attachments from the tibia (shinbone). Its specific causes are not known, but its most frequent occurrence in ballet seems to follow dancing on a hard floor (one reason why cement-floored studios are a bad idea) or landing incorrectly from jumps (heels off the floor and/or without a *demi-plié*). Preventive tactics include careful pre-*barre* warm-ups that emphasize gentle stretching of the calf muscles and foot flexors. Two exercises recommended are

1. Press the heels to the floor and, keeping the legs and back straight, lean forward to take hold of a wall or the *barre;* remain in this position sixty seconds.
2. *Demi-pliés* and *relevés* performed with or without turnout.

Following class, a repetition of the first exercise is advised, plus the following stretch:

> Stand on one leg and bend the other leg back at the knee, taking hold of that foot and keeping the knees near one another. Space should remain between the heel and the buttock to protect the knee. Hold for sixty seconds; repeat with the other leg.

Pain from shin splints can be severe, and the usual treatment, though not always effective, is simply heat and rest. Occasionally, a half-inch thick sponge-rubber pad worn inside the heel of the shoe gives relief; arch supports or tape around the shins may be advisable in particular cases. Dancers subject to shin splints should consult a physiotherapist for specific exercises to help

Stretching exercises
to help prevent shin splints

strengthen the muscles involved. If pain and local tenderness persist, they may signal a stress fracture, a serious problem that requires a physician's attention.

TENDONITIS

Tendonitis is an inflammation of a tendon, its connective tissue, or its sheath, the latter normally secreting a protective lubricant. If this lubricant is defective, then pain may result after repeated motions involving a given tendon. Overwork of the connecting muscle or a severe blow to a tendon may cause tendonitis, or the cause may be idiopathic—that is, unknown. Unfortunately, the Achilles tendon, connecting the back of the heel and the calf muscles, is particularly vulnerable to strain and thus is a not uncommon site for inflammation for dancers. The most effective treatment is rest—a hard prescription for most dancers to follow—but if it is ignored, the tendon problem may continue much longer than necessary. Because the application of heat may provoke more pain, ice may be more satisfactory, but so also may contrast baths of hot and cold water in some cases. Certainly a physician should be consulted, and taping of the tendon by a specialist or heel lifts inserted in the shoes may be effective, along with rest.

KNEE INJURIES

Persistent pain, redness, or swelling in the region of the knee are warning signs of a significant problem, perhaps a sprain of the ligaments around the knee or a case of tendonitis. Other serious symptoms are a tendency for the knee to lock or to give way suddenly, or to be unable to straighten fully, any one of which may indicate a cartilage tear or the slipping of the patella. An orthopedic physician should be consulted for accurate diagnosis and treatment.

The student must constantly be aware of the possible hazards to knees if circular movements (*ronds de jambes*) and knee bends (*demi-* and *grands pliés*) are practiced incorrectly. A knee is strongest when straight, therefore *rond de jambe à terre* practiced incorrectly with a relaxed knee invites stress to the surrounding ligaments. Closing to a tight fifth position *demi-plié* and then straightening the knees in that position can result in twisting the knees, especially if true outward rotation is not occurring at the hip joint. "Sitting" in a *grand plié* or allowing the knees to fall inward when rising out of a *plié* also contribute to stresses on the knee joint.

BACK AILMENTS

Back pain most common to dancers is caused by muscle strain, accentuated by rotary or bending movements of the back. A female dancer may experience such strain in the lower back when incorrectly attempting a high *arabesque*, hollowing out the low, lumbar area rather than distributing the extension throughout the spine. A male dancer may find he has pain higher in the back as a result of lifting his partner when the lift was made off balance without his center of gravity over his feet or when fatigued. Muscle spasm in the back may be a signal of such hazardous activity. Application of ice massage and gradual stretching may give relief. If strain has occurred, rest is the best remedy, followed by carefully selected back exercises.

A ruptured disc may also follow bending or lifting. Here the pain usually occurs quite low in the back and/or down the legs because the last two discs are the ones most commonly affected. Correct diagnosis between disc disease and muscle strain is sometimes difficult and requires considerable medical experience.

CLICKS

Painless "clicks" or snaps in the joints of the hips, knees, or ankles are often disturbing to students, who wonder whether they are doing something wrong. The answer, usually, is no; the sound indicates a bone rubbing against an unyielding tendon or ligament. When the leg is lifted high to the side (*grands battements* or *développés à la seconde*), a clicking can occur in the hip. Most common to late teenagers, it later disappears, apparently after more hip flexibility is achieved. Other clicks—in the ankles, for instance—may be present always. A painful click in the knee, however, may indicate cartilage damage.

CARE OF THE FEET

No part of the body must meet as many demands from ballet as the foot, which is asked to assume positions and perform movements quite outside its usual range. In spite of these unusual requirements, if a student assumes correct ballet positions and performs ballet movements correctly, the feet will be held in the proper anatomic position and will work as very effective levers.

Ballet feet must be strong and flexible; therefore, a dancer's training must produce both strength and suppleness in the feet. The ideal foot for ballet training would have roundish toes, all of medium length; an ankle that moves freely, allowing the foot when flexed to form a right angle to the leg, and when pointed to form a straight line from toe to hip; and, for a beginning student, a medium arch (the highly arched, slender foot, although beautiful when pointed, may indicate weakness).

The foot is a complicated mechanism consisting of twenty-six bones held together by a system of ligaments forming arches (the inside and outside longitudinal and the transverse, or metatarsal), which are supported by muscles. Its inherent (and inherited) shape is extremely important, but it will change after years of ballet study. Because particular demands are made of the female foot in point work, the following prerequisites should be met before a student goes on point: (1) the completion of a minimum of two or three years of basic ballet training; (2) correct posture when standing *and* moving; (3) correct performance of all exercises on *demi-pointe* (supporting knee absolutely straight, feet free from any tendency to sickle in or out); (4) a minimum age of twelve.

The last requirement is as important for parents and teachers to consider as it is frustrating for aspiring ballerinas or overly ambitious parents to follow. The reason is clear, however; ossification (the process of bone formation) of the feet is not sufficient in most children under twelve to withstand the strain imposed on the still unsolidified bones by standing or dancing on the toes. Serious deformities or injuries may result.

FOOT DISORDERS

Bunions: A swelling at the first joint of the big toe, caused by inflammation and thickening of a bursa, is commonly called a bunion. The foot that has a tendency to bunion formation (often determined by looking at the feet of parents or siblings) will, in all probability, develop one in intensive ballet training, although careful training often ensures correct functioning of the foot in spite of its abnormal appearance. However, extreme care should be given to the selection of proper-fitting ballet shoes (see page 49) and sensible, well-fitting street shoes. Moist heat applied before class and ice afterwards may alleviate some discomfort from an angered bunion.

Flat Feet: The clinical flat foot is weak, has no arch, and will never serve a dancer. However, a flexible foot may appear to be flat when bearing weight but will show an arch when weight is removed. Such a foot must be disciplined not to "roll" when assuming ballet positions. This muscle conditioning sometimes produces discomfort along the inner border of the foot. It is not serious, but when it persists, a few days' rest is advised. When work is resumed, care must be taken that the student does not attempt to turn out beyond correct range. Special muscle-strengthening exercises may be recommended, including lots of *battements tendus* to develop the set of short muscles on the underside of the foot.

MINOR FOOT AILMENTS

Professional dancers assume great fortitude toward blisters, corns, and other occupational foot nuisances, which, of course, are encountered by many people who never danced a step in their lives (ill-fitting nylons or street shoes can be a source of trouble for any pair of feet).

Dance students usually exist on a very limited budget, spending most of what extra money they have on ballet lessons and ballet shoes. Seeking professional treatment of foot problems is a luxury in which the student seldom indulges, unless and until a problem becomes acute. Some practical suggestions are offered for the prevention and treatment of minor disorders that may occur.

Blisters: Caused by excessive friction on a given area, blisters are best prevented by protecting the skin; that is, minimally, wearing ballet tights with feet (not ankle-length tights unless adequate socks are worn). Additional aids can be gauze pads, moleskin, or Band-Aids placed on the vulnerable site before the blister appears. Tender feet can be toughened by regular applications of tincture of benzoin and pampered by systematic use of talcum powder rubbed around the toes.

Sometimes a small blister need not be opened (thereby inviting the possibility of infection) but simply protected by a doughnut-shaped pad, the center of which can be filled with vaseline. When a sizable blister occurs, the area should be cleansed with an antiseptic; the blister should be carefully drained—opened, that is, with a sterile needle (which has been boiled or held in a flame); the wound should be painted with iodine and covered with a sterile gauze pad. Blisters that have been unroofed—that is, the overlying skin removed, thus exposing a tender area—heal more slowly. They must be carefully treated with an antiseptic and covered with a sterile pad to avoid the greater possibility of infection.

Soft Corns: Soft corns between the toes occur as a result of excessive pressure. Precautions include foam-rubber wedges or bunches of lamb's wool placed between the toes—but do not encircle them, as that might cut off the circulation.

Hard Corns: The prevention of hard corns is ultimately the elimination of the pressures that cause them (sometimes improper footwear). If the problem persists—and it often does for dancers on point—the least that the victim can do is to wear simple pads or moleskin, adhesive felt, or foam that are designed to disperse the pressure from the area. Horseshoe-shaped pads that do not cover the corn itself should be used in preference to circular (life buoy-shaped) ones, as the flesh eventually will work through the hole when the latter are used.

Corns on the ball of the foot can reflect a mechanical problem of the toe and/or metatarsal head and can be difficult to eliminate. A total understanding of the cause requires study by a professional podiatrist, who should also be the one to trim a corn.

Callouses: Callouses are usually protective devices—and very effective ones in the dancer's case. If the buildup of tissue becomes too great, simple abrasives can be used—callous file or pumice stone. Cracks or fissures can best be prevented by keeping the feet clean, by limiting the callous buildup, and by using a lubricant (Vaseline, baby oil, or the like).

Toenail Problems: Long toenails can cause trouble for dancers in soft ballet shoes, but most especially for dancers on point. Most dancers keep their nails cut much shorter than the average person does. Proper pedicure should conform to the contour of the toe, not to a line straight across, as toenail growth follows individual patterns. If, in spite of proper care, ingrown nails persist, they may be caused by improper shoes, or possibly an inherited tendency. An operation that removes the nail plate and the deformed root portion is sometimes advised. Some relief can be obtained by soaking the foot for short periods several times a day in hot water and by placing a small amount of lamb's wool beneath the toenail edge.

Thickened nails can be caused by injury or fungous disease. They must be either thinned continually by the use of grinding devices or surgically removed (along with the root, which causes the problem). Dancers who do a great deal of point work often develop one or two thickened nails, which usually cure themselves by dropping off, revealing a new, normal nail underneath.

Fungus: No one cures fungus (the cause of athlete's foot, among other things), but it can be managed easily with fungicides. People apparently either have a tendency for fungus or not, and if they have and once become infected, then the potential is always present.

Plantar Warts: Plantar warts are caused by a virus and occur on the *planta* or sole of the foot. The discomfort from a wart on a weight-bearing area of the foot can be a very real concern to a dancer. Surgical removal of plantar warts can keep dancers off their feet for many days, and, in severe cases, for weeks or months. Better to have the warts treated chemically, a method frequently used by dermatologists, because dance activity can continue normally during such treatment.

EVERYDAY CARE OF THE FEET

Healthy feet must be clean. They should be thoroughly washed and carefully dried, especially between the toes. An absorbent foot powder should be used if the feet perspire. Tired feet can be revived by baths of contrasting temperatures—hot to cold to hot. . . . (The addition of Epsom salts to foot baths is probably of no value.) Long soaking should be avoided as it can cause cracks between the toes. Elevation of the feet can offer respite by reducing the amount of blood in the extremities.

EATING HABITS

Almost all dancers have, or think they have, a weight problem. They are concerned with the importance of creating a certain image on stage, where lights and costumes have the effect of adding pounds to the body, and dancers and dance students rightly conclude that steps of elevation and point work are much easier to perform, and are less stressful to the anatomy, when the body does not carry excess weight. Dancers view their bodies as instruments of expression, as a violinist might view a violin. But, in their zeal to stay thinner than would seem necessary by most ordinary standards, dancers and dance students sometimes ignore the fact that their bodies were designed for purposes other than dancing. The demands and expectations made of the human instrument, the dancer's body, require necessary nutrients every day to produce good health, consistent energy, and a sense of well-being. In dealing with problems of overweight and fears of gaining weight, dancers must consider the quality of food as well as the quantity.

DIET

Diet must be based on many things, including height, sex, age, metabolic rate, and bone structure. No dancer or dance student should attempt a self-prescribed "crash" diet (which often leaves one tense, tired, and prone to illness and injury) or rely on tricky diet pills to control appetite artificially (weight thus lost often is regained as soon as the pills are stopped). Fad diets, although frequently the subject of dressing-room conversations ("I eat *nothing* but yogurt and celery"), are not the answer either as no single food contains anywhere near the fifty essential nutrients required for a healthy body.

If an overweight (or underweight) condition exists, it deserves the attention of a professional person who can prescribe a particular, corrective diet. Rather than a schedule of regimented menus, diet, to the dancer, should mean a habitual way of eating so that the body maintains itself with maximum energy and efficiency.

NUTRITION

A person subject to listlessness, frequent illness, and a generally low energy level, may be suffering from poor nutrition. Just consuming a certain number of calories every day is no guarantee of good nutrition. Calories are the measure of energy released by the food a person eats, and the amount differs according to the kind of food. But any food should also provide a variety of substances—nutrients that are essential for the building, upkeep, and repair of tissues, and for the efficient functioning of the body. According to their use, nutrients may be classified as proteins (for body maintenance and growth), carbohydrates (for the most efficient energy fuel), fats (for some energy fuel and essential vitamins and fatty acids), and specific vitamins and minerals (for transformation of energy and regulation of metabolic functions).

Efficient intake of food is essential to the healthy functioning of any animal, and improper nutrition can lead to loss or gain of weight, lack of energy, and a number of diseases. Like other people who participate in active physical effort, dancers can observe a very direct connection between what is ingested into their bodies and their performing condition. Of particular importance is the maintaining and replenishing of body fluid.

> It is of the utmost importance to maintain a good state of hydration by adequate intake of salt and water, particularly in warm, humid studios and in periods of heat acclimation. Dehydration compromises energy metabolism and limits endurance, and can be life threatening if extreme. Obviously, water pills (diuretics) for weight loss only compound the dehydration, potassium loss, and muscle weakness, and should never be used. Nor are other pills, such as stimulants, ever indicated in the dancer either for purposes for stifling appetite or combating fatigue.[4]

The minimum daily requirement of vitamins and minerals is sometimes a point of controversy. Many people, including most dancers, supplement their daily menu with extra doses of vitamins, especially C and E. It is thought that women may need additional iron in their diet because of the loss of blood during menstruation. But it should be remembered not only that these vitamins and minerals occur naturally in foods but that their supplements are no substitute for natural food. A well-balanced, nutritious diet is essential, and it may be totally adequate for the body's vitamin-mineral needs.

ENERGY FOODS

The day's first meal should contribute to the energy needed for classes and rehearsals that follow. Thus, breakfast might be two slices of whole-grain toast with either half a cup of low-fat cottage cheese or a boiled or poached egg. Dancers in a hurry can quickly prepare a healthful drink of one cup low-fat milk blended with one-eighth cup powdered brewer's yeast—*not* baker's yeast—flavored with a banana, concentrated orange juice, or nutmeg. Granola-type cereal or wheat germ or oatmeal with a helping of fruit and low-fat milk are other quick choices. Remember, cold foods are as nourishing as hot foods and almost anything eaten for breakfast is better than nothing.

Recent diet research places greater emphasis on the energy-producing qualities of carbohydrates than on the more traditional protein sources. Thus, a preperformance meal of pasta is more beneficial than one of steak. Dancers and dance students often are forced into unusual eating schedules. Ideally, their preclass or preperformance meal should be eaten three hours before the activity in order to allow time for digestion and absorption of the food. Since this is not always possible, several light meals a day (eaten one to one and a half hours before the dance event) may have to be substituted for three normal meals. Instead of high-calorie, low-nutrient food such as potato chips, soft drinks, or candy bars, consider the following foods for inclusion in easily prepared, nutritious mini-meals:

Hard-boiled eggs
Yogurt in small carton
Cheese
Tiger's milk in powdered form to be mixed in one-serving shaker with milk
Fresh fruit
Raw vegetable pieces: carrots, celery, small tomatoes, cucumbers, turnips
Individual containers of unsweetened fruit and vegetable juices
Celery stuffed with peanut butter, ham salad, etc.
Handful of alfalfa sprouts
Peanut butter/granola squares (instant protein powder can be added)
Peanut butter or cashew butter spread on rye crisp–type crackers
Peanut butter mixed with protein powder or brewer's yeast and spread on graham crackers
Wheat germ or granola with milk
Whole-grain sandwiches
Seeds: sunflower, pumpkin, roasted soybeans
Nuts: all kinds

NOTES

1. Celia Sparger, *Ballet Physique* (London: Adam & Charles Black, 1958), 10.
2. Celia Sparger, *Anatomy and Ballet* (London: Adam & Charles Black, 1982), 10.
3. For an introduction to some of the better-known body therapies and how they may contribute to improved patterns of movement or to speedier recovery from injury, see the series of articles, "Body Therapies and the Modern Dancer," by Martha Myers in *Dance Magazine* (August 1983). Among the movement systems and therapies briefly discussed are Irmgard Bartenieff's "Fundamentals," the "Alexander Technique" of Frederick Matthias Alexander, Moshe Feldenkrais's "Awareness Through Movement," and the theories of "Ideokinesis" developed by Mabel Todd and Lulu Sweigard.
4. L. M. Vincent, M.D., *The Dancer's Book of Health* (New York: Andrews and McMeel, 1978), 135.

CHAPTER 7
THE BALLET PROFESSION

The college freshman who begins the study of ballet must realize that at that same age most dancers who aspire to a professional performing career are already fairly accomplished technicians, having had seven or eight years of training, and are frequently already employed by a professional company. Adults who begin ballet training in their early thirties must acknowledge that many professional dancers consider retiring from the stage well before forty. What sort of life do these artists live, whose careers begin and end so early?

The present chapter offers a glimpse of the professional dancer in training and at work, and it gives the parents of would-be dancers some idea of how to start children in ballet. Also discussed are some areas of the theatre that even the late-starting dancer may encounter as a member of a civic, a regional, or even a semiprofessional dance company. Mention is made of other ballet-related careers, many that are new since the "dance boom" of the past two decades.

THE YOUNG DANCER

The child who develops an interest in serious ballet study has very likely already enjoyed classes in some sort of creative dance or pre-ballet. By age ten the physique, mind, and emotions are considered grown up enough to withstand the rigors of ballet and the child will start going to class twice a week, probably one afternoon and Saturday morning. Soon, as classes become more frequent, they invariably will seem to get in the way of other exciting social or school-sponsored events. The dedicated youngster learns early that painful, unpopular sacrifices will have to be made in order to attend daily dance classes.

The ballet emphasis on the body's capacity for a large range of movement requires training at an early age, when greater lengthening and limbering of the muscles can occur, a training, moreover, not provided by sports activities.

Difficult decisions face both young students and their parents, partly because there is no assurance how far the child's talent will develop, how long the child's interest will last, or whether—after all the work, sweat, tears, money, and sacrifices—any concrete reward (a contract with a ballet company) will be forthcoming. The uncertainty of ending up with a dance job even after years of training and, for a boy at least, the nagging reality that probably greater pay, prestige, and security could be achieved in almost any other field (plus the lingering, nineteenth-century notion that ballet is essentially a feminine art) are so persuasive to American parents that they seldom let a son begin ballet lessons, much less encourage him to prepare for a career as a dancer. Therefore, American boys tend to begin ballet study at a later age than girls, and at a time when they are less dependent on their parents.[1]

Although a few schools offer both dance training and an accredited academic curriculum for grade school through high school, serious ballet students who live anywhere but in a few large cities usually must prepare as best they can. Fortunately, many excellent teachers and schools can be found throughout the country.

The quality of a school can be ascertained by getting an expert's opinion, by visiting the school—even untrained eyes often can tell something about the quality of a dance class, and by making inquiries about the teacher's own ballet background. Such information may be sought from or corroborated by someone in the dance profession, perhaps at a nearby college or university. Civic and regional companies often can suggest schools associated with their organizations, but even these can range from excellent to barely adequate. One concrete criterion is: When does the teacher allow a student to go on point? If there are six-year-olds tottering around in point shoes, then the school must be avoided—and should be closed down (see page 137). Even if point work is not started until age twelve, have there been at least two preceding years of careful work, and do students look straight when on point? If they sag—lower back hollowed out, knees wobbly, ankles rolling in or out—then they are not ready, and thoughtful students will go elsewhere.

PROFESSIONAL PREPARATION

As a rule, by age seventeen or eighteen (that is, immediately after high school graduation), students with career aspirations will enter a professional ballet school. The training there may not be any finer than at the hometown or neighborhood studio (and possibly not as good because of overcrowded conditions in some professional schools). However, students will benefit from having their talents appraised by people in the profession and from seeing themselves in close comparison with the products of the professional schools. By taking classes from a school associated with a company, students will know when company replacements are needed, when annual or semiannual auditions are scheduled, and when the school faculty thinks they are ready to take the audition.

There are other routes. A student can write to a company to request an audition, or sometimes auditions can be arranged when a company visits a town while on tour. Members of a touring company may spot a talent in a local studio; some companies conduct regular summer workshops that can serve as showcases for aspiring performers. Some students may elect to enter a university that offers a major in ballet and performing opportunities in campus-based or local companies.

But the surest way into the more prestigious professional ballet companies has come to be through the professional school associated with a given company. Companies like to mold their dancers into a common style and groom their soloists for the many roles in the repertory. Therefore, they would give preference to a talented eighteen-year-old who can be enrolled in their professional school, rather than to an equally talented twenty-two-year-old who has already finished training elsewhere. In many cases, such as the National Ballet of Canada or the New York City Ballet, a company can oversee the entire preparatory period, from beginning children's classes to preprofessional ones. Graduation performances often are exciting concerts that are reviewed by critics, with an invitation to join the resident company extended to some lucky graduates.

Because the performing years are short, the ballet business must be entered early. Twenty years is considered a reasonable period for peak performance, even though stars may continue to enchant audiences well beyond that limit, as in the cases of Fonteyn, Ulanova, and Alicia Alonso. Even so, statistics have shown that most company dancers are under age thirty.[2]

A traditional gateway to membership in a company has been by audition. Any audition requires patience—patience to wait one's turn, trying to keep muscles warm and enthusiasm at a high pitch, while others are being judged; patience to stand for interminable minutes in a line next to other eager bodies, all the while being critically surveyed and evaluated according to the immediate, undisclosed needs of the company; patience to wait for another audition or possible openings in the company later on, if a first audition is unsuccessful.

An audition requires a certain protocol. Mamas, teachers, friends should be left at home. Stage makeup should not be worn; an audition is not a performance. Applicants should be dressed neatly and simply, as for a ballet class. They should come to the audition fully warmed up, able to dance the first combinations as well as possible, for there may never be a chance for later ones. The applicant should do exactly what the choreographer asks without adding personal variations. Following precise instructions, and quickly, is a requisite for the professional theatre. It is a good idea to be prepared to perform a short solo or variation.

Nervousness is to be expected. But a body that has been well trained will not be destroyed by butterflies in the stomach. The carriage of the arms, the shape of the legs, the flexibility of the spine, the arch of the foot will remain, even if accompanied by a tense face or wobbly balance. The judges are professionals, but they, too, once had to audition for a first time, and they can recognize talent and training beneath a nervous skin.

Unfortunately, talent, good training, a reasonably attractive face, and a well-proportioned body are not guarantees of success at an audition. The supply of dancers with those qualities is much greater than the availability of positions in professional ballet companies. (Troupes that offer year-round employment in the United States are still relatively rare—perhaps a dozen or so at any one time.) Dancers often attribute their success (or more usually their lack of success) to politics (whom one knows) and luck (being in the right place at the right time).

JOINING A COMPANY

The dancer who is successful at an audition will enter a relatively small, intimate community. Most United States ballet companies have fewer than thirty dancers, even though the "big two," American Ballet Theatre and New York City Ballet, have close to one hundred on their rosters. A company is headed by an artistic director—usually a choreographer, perhaps the chief one of the troupe—who, in consultation with the business administration of the company, makes all final decisions—repertory, promotions, hiring, firing. There may be associate or assistant directors. There will be a ballet master or mistress whose duties include rehearsing ballets and giving classes to company dancers.

The new member of the company will begin a daily regimen that, by most ordinary work standards, is strangely cloistered and far removed from the "real" world. It begins each day with class, a period of hard physical work, heavy breathing, and sweat-soaked practice clothes. Every dancer, no matter how experienced, must do daily *pliés*, *battements*, and *ronds de jambes*. It is a humbling experience, for without the grueling, daily exercises, no dancer's body will retain the strength and precision necessary for ballet performance, nor will technique improve.

BALLET REHEARSAL

The class systematically warms up the dancer's body for the rehearsal period, which often follows directly. A dancer may spend two to five hours daily in rehearsals (sometimes more, for which overtime compensation is generally paid), and these may be called with little prior warning; dancers regulate their lives by notices on the rehearsal bulletin board.

At a rehearsal for a new ballet, it is the choreographer who is in charge and who is given the power to cast and compose the ballet of his or her choice. These decisions must, of course, meet with the approval of the company director, but choreographers are entrusted with a great deal of power. How does one compose a dance? Ask a choreographer and receive a very personal answer; one method may work for one and quite another method for the next. Even the same choreographer may use different strategies with different ballets or dancers. The music for the ballet or the idea of the ballet may have whirred around in the choreographer's head for weeks, months, or years, but a first rehearsal sometimes produces only the most tenuous promise of what will develop. Some choreographers arrive at a rehearsal with notepads full of explicit details for gestures, movements, and floor patterns; others prefer to experiment there, letting chance happenings or even accidents suggest movement possibilities. All must respond to the particular qualities of the dancers assembled for their ballet. Even if the choreographic process appears random, it usually is following the broad, basic structure of the dance as it has been viewed time and time again in the mind of the choreographer.

Almost without exception, choreographers for professional ballet companies are former dancers themselves, and most of them therefore learned the craft of choreography by apprenticeship, watching a master choreographer at work while they participated as dancers in the creation of a new ballet. This background enables choreographers to draw upon a large movement vocabulary, which they then are able to demonstrate. One choreographer may expect the cast to imitate movements exactly; another may merely indicate the desired movement in the barest outline, preferring to see how the dancers themselves continue and fulfill the movement. A rehearsal can be an exciting creative experience for all concerned.

Once the details are worked out for each dance sequence, they are practiced over and over again. Some choreographers never change a single step once it has been set, but others redo, throw out, start again. During rehearsals for a new ballet, a dancer learns to keep several versions of one sequence in memory—a prodigious task, because the same dancer will have roles to remember and perform in many other ballets. Beginning students are wise to cultivate dance "memory" as they are learning dance technique: Try to reconstruct an entire class by memory. Practice doing this every day while the experience of dancing is still fresh. Eventually a dancer's muscles provide a memory storehouse; they seem to respond without conscious mental effort.

Human memory and word of mouth have been the links between the choreography of one generation and the dancers of the next, although today more and more use is being made of video tape and dance notation (see page 152). A skilled dance notator is a valuable asset for the preservation of a company repertory and the establishment of a choreographic library. But, the rare dancer (and there are a few) whose memory can recall every step of every dancer in a given ballet is still a most treasured member of the fleeting world of ballet.

Another valuable member of any ballet company is the rehearsal pianist, who may sit for hours replaying the same short passage of music until a choreographic problem has been solved and the sequence learned by the dancers. When a reliable pianist is not available, a choreographer may rehearse with a tape recorder. Of, if music is being composed especially for ballet, the dancers may hear only counts at rehearsal. Because of every-increasing production and rehearsal costs, a complete orchestral score may not be heard and practiced to before the first stage rehearsal.

In all cases, counting of the musical bars or phrases is done in great detail by dancers and choreographers alike; very, very seldom is any movement improvised on the ballet stage. Even large crowd scenes in some of the classical ballets are planned down to minute details of who goes where and when and how. New stages call for adjustments, and sometimes particular movements will need to be modified or changed, of course, but these revisions are worked out before performance, not during it. Stage rehearsals are tedious but necessary parts of the dancer's life. Before the initial performance of any ballet, it must be seen on stage, costumes must be danced in, lighting plans must be tried, and the orchestra must be rehearsed with the dancers.

Companies that tour extensively learn to adapt to all kinds of theatre conditions. They are likely to find a differently proportioned stage at every stop—wide and shallow, narrow and deep, square, semicircular—and theatres with skimpy wings making leaping exits hazardous at best.

A dancer's sense of space becomes finely tuned. Relationships to other dancers must be kept, and distances from the sides or front or back of the stage must be preserved. This is not accomplished with a yardstick or the counting of floorboards, although visual aids can include such visible features as an auditorium's lighted exit signs, aisles, or openings into the wings. But through training during rehearsals dancers learn to relate quickly to distances and to remember spatial patterns.

Occasionally a company on tour will arrive at a new theatre with insufficient time to rehearse the evening's performance fully. The best they can do is to "block" the dances on the new stage, the dancers walking through their parts and, by means of a kind of elaborate hand and finger sign language, indicating the steps that later will be performed in those spots.

BALLET PERFORMANCE

Backstage, the stage manager or *regisseur* tries to oversee the preperformance activity that, to a visitor, may resemble chaos. Stagehands lug equipment, scenery, and props around. Lighting technicians preside over a maze of wires and towers (light "trees"). Wardrobe ladies, mouths full of pins, may be making last-minute alterations. Each person does his or her specific job; union regulations forbid the overlapping of backstage tasks. Amid the dust and drafts and commotion, the dancers, bundled in layers of wool, go through *barre* exercises, holding onto any wall or chair or ladder available.

Where is the magic that will soon be seen on stage? It is slowly forming in the minds and muscles of the dancers. The ritual of warming up is only one of several that prepare the dancers for performance and preoccupy the nerves. Makeup is another. Dancers no longer wear masks, but they cover their everyday faces with carefully applied stage makeup. It is more elaborate than that used by other stage artists, because it must stand up under the rigors of fast movement, varied lighting, and profuse perspiration.

For women there is another ritual—that of preparing point shoes. Many minutes backstage are spent inspecting and cleaning the shoes. Some dancers also use this time to darn the points of the shoes, making little pads of delicate stitches, which can lengthen the life of the shoes and give them greater traction on the floor. Long before a performance, each dancer has personally sewn on the ribbons of her shoes and broken in each pair according to her own method—ranging from simply walking around in the shoes, to soaking them in water, to slamming a door on them (when off the feet, of course!). The "box" of the shoe is in reality only several layers of cloth held together by a strong glue. The rest of the support comes from a leather sole and shank. Point shoes break in easily and their life is short. A ballerina may use a new pair of shoes for each act of a ballet; a member of the *corps de ballet* may have to make do with only one new pair a week. Shoes are provided by the company, and they usually are built according to a mold of the dancer's foot made by one of a handful of dance shoe manufacturers.

As curtain time approaches, the dancers help zip or hook each other into their costumes. Hairdos are given a final layer of spray. Toe shoe ribbons are checked for the twentieth time (a loose ribbon is a dancer's nightmare). *Demi-pliés* and *battements tendus* keep pace with the flutter in the stomach. Nervousness can attack the dance novice and dance veteran alike, but most, probably all, pride themselves on being troupers. They know that their nerves are bringing their bodies to the high pitch necessary for performance.

LOOKING AT THE BALLET

What does the audience see as the curtain opens? The merely interested but ballet-uneducated public will immediately see movement with a capital M, for that is the prime of ballet. They will see living sculpture created by a lifted leg and an outstretched arm—and the spaces framed by those limbs that become important designs in themselves. Members of an audience may not know whether a movement is done correctly, but they can sense its quality. Fellow humans are dancing, often expressing human feelings in dramatic situations, and the emotions and muscles of the audience are touched empathically. Costumes and stage designs help set the appropriate scene; lighting underscores the appropriate mood. Above all, the music is linked to the spectacle on the stage. Some, or all, of these elements are employed—even in a so-called abstract ballet—to carry the audience along a choreographer's intended path.

Ballet enthusiasts (known as balletomanes) analyze all the elements, sometimes exhibiting peculiar delight in dissecting minute details of a performance. They argue the merits of one dancer over another in a given role, or view a ballet in the light of some rumor about the choreographer's personal life or a current company intrigue. Included in the group of observers are the ballet critics. If those functionaries have any advantage over the ordinary public, it is that they have attended a great many more ballet performances, thereby gaining some yardstick with which to measure one evening or one ballet trend against another. Still, critics are human and will express their personal preferences. Cyril Beaumont, a prolific and oft-quoted writer on dance, admits that ballet criticism is "the examination of a choreographic work in the light of an informed taste which is part intellectual and part emotional."[3]

The repertory offered to ballet critics and audiences essentially represents three historical periods. Greatly simplified, these divisions are the nineteenth century (the full-length, story-ballets), the early twentieth century (the one-act ballet "miniatures"), and the contemporary period (the ever more eclectic works since the 1930s). Great variation exists within each period, of course, and each offers particular delights to, and requires particular awareness from, the viewer. An acquaintance with ballet history is essential for "an informed taste" for critic and patron alike.

Reviewing the New York dance scene, critic Marcia B. Siegel observes:

> Seeing is a very selective, individual and concrete process, and it means more to me than opinion. . . . Each separate dance experience carries its own unique and momentary life, but to consider *only* that singular evening's lifetime, it seems to me, is to deny evolution, to deny civilization.[4]

A dancer can inevitably and almost instantly sense an audience's approval or disapproval, its involvement or its boredom. Audience reactions can change during the course of an evening, and it is the performer's particular pleasure to change indifference to enthusiasm. An audience's support, with appropriate laughter or hushness, is intoxicating to the performer, who may receive the final tribute of applause in a state of inward jubilation but outward calm.

AFTER THE SHOW

Coming down from the high emotional pitch of a performance is not easy. A dancer may long to repeat the whole show immediately. The body is warm and loose, the nerves are calm, the unknown has been faced and conquered. Now, one could really perform! No thrill, physical or spiritual, could compare with those moments of power onstage—pity the person who is not a dancer!

Backstage, chatter is almost exclusively about the performance that has just ended. The dancers, unwilling to let go of the magic they have created, must nevertheless get back to reality. Costumes must be hung, faces must be cleansed of all makeup, bags must be packed. The dancer's body, which has just spent several hours fluctuating between near exhaustion and instant recovery, cries out for food and drink. The company heads for a late-night restaurant or to a reception that a local organization may have prepared in their honor. Deprived of stage makeup and colored lights, the dancers look appallingly pale and much smaller than they did on stage. But these people are athletes, even though they are trained to conceal all effort, and when the night's work is finished, they need to replenish their bodies with an ample meal.

Dancers realize that they live in a separate world. They grew up in ballet classrooms; they were socialized in studio dressing rooms and rehearsal halls. As professionals, their six-day-a-week schedule permits them little time for interests or friends outside the dance profession; it even permits them little sunshine. They are like hardy indoor houseplants who thrive under artificial lights—of the theatre.

Robert Weiss, a principal dancer with New York City Ballet, speaks of the dancer's commitment:

> It's a very funny profession. . . . You get into it at such a young age. . . . It's not only a profession, it's a way of life. . . . Despite all the problems, mental and physical, the company politics and all that stuff, there's a reward in dancing that's indescribable. It's just different from any of the other performing arts—the mental and physical coming together. And when everything is right—two or three times a year, maybe—well . . . there's no other feeling like it and you remember that and you'll do almost anything to feel that again.[5]

Onstage, dancers are magicians; offstage, they tend to be supremely disciplined, practical, punctual people. The fairy princess leaves the theatre, returning home (or back to her hotel room) to do the inevitable evening laundry of sweaty leotards and tights. She looks forward to such simple luxuries as a hot bath and a night's sleep as few others can appreciate. Is this a "real" life? What of the future? Next year or the next? The tired dancer focuses on tomorrow. There is class to take at ten-thirty in the morning.

OTHER BALLET-RELATED CAREERS

The traditional route to the professional stage, as just described, is not possible for the adult beginner, but other interesting paths exist, and many new ones are opening. The increasing popularity of dance in general has created the need for knowledgeable experts in numerous ballet-related fields, now located in many parts of the country besides the large dance centers of the east and west coasts.

TEACHING AND CHOREOGRAPHY

Teaching and choreographing are two traditional nonperforming careers that immediately come to mind. Both require an intensive dance background, but not necessarily a professional performing one. University and college dance curricula vary, but most offer courses in choreography ("composition classes") and teacher training ("methods classes"). The latter usually is geared toward public school teaching (dance has enjoyed a significant increase in elementary and secondary schools) and college programs (where a master's degree is routinely expected for a faculty appointment, especially in lieu of professional dance experience).

Career preparation for private studio teaching has been haphazard in the United States, where no certification or licensing requirements obtain. Yet the challenges of running a commercial studio call for a careful program of study:

> Whether offered by a university, a conservatory or a professional studio, such a program should require studies in a variety of dance techniques with special emphasis on teaching beginners and preschool creative movement. It should require instruction in preparing course outlines spanning a greater number of development years than most public school or university teachers face when dealing with the progress of a single student. Curriculum planning would need to identify long-range goals as well as detail the construction of daily, monthly and yearly class plans which allow for physically sound and emotionally satisfying progression in technique and also some initial experience in composition for the student. Selection of accompaniment, improvisation, creating combinations and studies for different levels to achieve specific technique goals, educational theory and instructional methods, child development, psychology, anatomy or physiology, choreography, production, studio organization, administration, promotion, business practices and financial management should all be a part of the studio teacher's preparation. A little advice on dealing with stage mothers and some basic professional ethics would not be amiss.[6]

RECORDING DANCE

Recording dance, either by special notation or by video tape and film, is an expanding field that offers great benefits to both the dance world and the community at large. Its purposes are

> to preserve masterworks for future generations; to increase the availability of the work beyond its immediate performance; to provide accurate tools for stylistic and structural analysis by the historian, critic, and researcher . . . ; to furnish students and choreographers with material for study. Anthropologists, ethnologists, and sociologists look at recorded movement for clues to the work habits and folk dances of other cultures.[7]

Skilled technicians, sensitive to the special requirements of the dance, are needed for preserving dance on film or video tape, as well as for compiling cassettes or filmstrips for instructional use. The popularity of dance on television and in movies creates a demand for better production by those industries.

As a method of recording dance, however, film or tape usually must be augmented by notation. Many methods have been tried and used since the fifteenth century. Today, the two notation systems most used are Labanotation (developed by Rudolf Laban and first published in 1928) and the Benesh method, also known as Choreology (developed in England in the 1950s).[8]

An increasing number of college dance programs offer courses in notation. Special training programs frequently are offered by the Dance Notation Bureau in New York City, which also secures work for many notators (those who write down movement in a notation system) and reconstructors (those who restage a notated dance). The use of the IBM Labanotation typewriter and experiments with computerized equipment make this an exciting, innovative field.

HISTORY, RESEARCH, AND CRITICISM

Reconstruction of dances from older types of notation has given recent impetus to the field of dance history, an endeavor that combines research, writing, and performance with knowledge of music, theatre, social customs, and dance. Thus, the Renaissance or Baroque dance scholar is in demand by early music festivals, art museums, libraries, theatre companies, and college dance, music, and drama departments. Ballet companies interested in reviving long-lost works have employed dance researchers and reconstructors to restore important dances to today's stages.[9] Such activity has helped establish respect for dance scholarship both within the profession and in educational academies. Training of dance writers, researchers, and critics is beginning to be found on more campuses. The establishment in 1982 of the first United States graduate program in dance history (at the Riverside campus of the University of California) is but one recent example. Other academic disciplines are recognizing certain dance courses (especially dance history) as arts and humanities options in general college requirements.

Newspapers and periodicals are featuring more dance articles, thus employing more writers and critics whose specialty is dance. The field itself needs more scholarly journals even as the number and price of published dance books seems ever escalating.

Dance scholars must have access to libraries. One of particular value is the Dance Collection of the New York Public Library. Located in the Performing Arts Research Center at Lincoln Center in New York City, the Dance Collection not only contains over 28,000 books and pamphlets relating to dance, but also manuscripts, periodicals, music scores, libretti, pictures and prints, original drawings and designs, programs and clippings, and a rapidly growing film and video tape collection.

THERAPY AND MEDICINE

Perhaps one of the greatest areas of growth in the field of related activities is dance therapy, a little-known profession prior to the 1940s even though dance and healing have been associated since ancient times. Today, the American Dance Therapy Association defines dance therapy as

> the psychotherapeutic use of movement as a process which furthers the emotional and physical integration of the individual.[10]

Those who may benefit are

> individuals who require special services because of behavioral, learning, perceptual and/or physical disorders; and rehabilitation of emotionally disturbed, physically handicapped, neurologically impaired and the socially deprived of all ages, in groups and individually.[11]

Both graduate and undergraduate degree programs in dance therapy allow academic specialization in this field, with workshops and special courses offering additional preparation.

Dance medicine, focusing on the special needs of dancers, has begun to attract doctors, some of whom are hired by professional dance companies. A great deal more scientific medical knowledge, testing, and publication would benefit our understanding of basic ballet principles—for example, the order and repetition of *barre* exercises.

ADMINISTRATION AND MANAGEMENT

Arts administration and management are areas of increasing need and diversity as companies, festivals, and programs seek funding and bookings, coordinate arts events and publicity, and deal with legal and budgetary matters. Training programs in arts management and administration include workshops as well as degree programs at universities, but many posts, because of their varied requirements, require on-the-job training.

PRODUCTION

Obvious performance-related fields include such vital areas as stage and theatre design, costuming and lighting, and music accompanying, composition, arranging, and conducting. The skilled technical director who can oversee these, and more, aspects of production is highly prized.

VOLUNTEER ASSISTANCE

Every dance organization benefits from well-informed, dance-loving people who may serve on boards of directors of companies, on the guilds of schools, or in a host of other service capacities connected with ballet production and education. The energy, ideas, and enthusiasm of such people provide invaluable assistance to the entire field of dance. Not the least important in this category are the informed, sympathetic members of the audience who regularly attend and support dance concerts. All these "volunteers" deserve a sincere bow of gratitude from the dance community.

As this brief discussion illustrates, there is more to the dance field than dance. But, no matter what ballet-related vocation (or avocation) is pursued, it is pursued best by persons who have had some dance training. So the first rule of preparation for any of these careers is: Buy some basic dance equipment (see pages 48–50), enroll in the best school available, and study ballet technique diligently (and perhaps other dance techniques as well). Make a habit of attending dance performances. When possible, join local or campus performing groups and participate (onstage or backstage) in theatre productions. Observe master teachers conducting technique, composition, or improvisation classes. Observe choreographers conducting rehearsals. These years of preparation can occur along with other training or other jobs, because such dance classes, rehearsals, and performances frequently take place in the evening or on weekends. Even when dreams of being a professional dancer are not the goal, one can pleasurably (and perhaps even profitably) take part in the world of ballet. Class just may begin at seven-thirty in the evening!

NOTES

1. Ronald Federico, "Recruitment, Training, and Performance: The Case for Ballet," in Phyllis Stewart and Muriel Cantor, eds. *Varieties of Work* (Boston: Schenkman, 1973). Federico's research is based on interviews with approximately one-half of all dancers in 1968 who were members of professional ballet companies in the United States. He reports that only eleven percent of his male respondents claimed to have been influenced toward dance training by their families, while fifty-four percent of women made this claim. Correlatively, eight-six percent of the females had begun ballet lessons by age eleven in contrast to only twenty-two percent of the males.
2. Federico, *ibid.*, reports that only eleven percent of his interviewees were under nineteen years of age and only thirteen percent were over twenty-nine, which suggests that fully three-quarters of all professional dance company members in the United States are in the age range of nineteen to twenty-nine.
3. Quoted in Katherine Sorley Walker, *Dance and Its Creators* (New York: John Day, 1972), 112.
4. Marcia B. Siegel, *Watching the Dance Go By* (Boston: Houghton Mifflin, 1977), xvi.
5. Quoted in *The Los Angeles Times*, 11 June 1981.
6. Mimi Marr, "Where Do They Go When the Dancing Stops?" *Dance Magazine* (September 1975), 64.
7. Linda Grandey and Nancy Reynolds, "Recording the Dance," *The Dance Catalogue*, ed. Nancy Reynolds (New York: Harmony Books, 1979), 194.

8. Two useful guides to these notation systems are: Rudolf and Joan Benesh, *An Introduction to Benesh Dance Notation* (London: Adam & Charles Black, 1965), and Ann Hutchinson, *Labanotation* (New York: Theatre Arts Books, 1977).
9. For instance, the Joffrey Ballet and the Sadler's Wells Royal Ballet have added to their repertory the 1847 *pas de six* from *La Vivandière*, choreographed (after Antonio Guerra) by Arthur Saint-Léon and recently reconstructed by Ann Hutchinson Guest from Saint-Léon's notation.
10. Kayla Kazahn Zalk, "Dance Therapy: The Oldest Form of Healing and a New Profession," *The Dance Catalogue*, ed. Nancy Reynolds (New York: Harmony Books, 1979), 205.
11. *Ibid.*

SELECTED READING

GENERAL REFERENCE

Balanchine, George, and Francis Mason. *101 Stories of the Great Ballets.* Garden City, N.Y.: Doubleday, Dolphin Books, 1975.

Brinson, Peter, and Clement Crisp. *Ballet and Dance: A Guide to the Repertory.* London: David & Charles, 1980.

Clark, Mary, and David Vaughan, eds. *The Encylopedia of Dance and Ballet.* New York: Putnam, 1977.

Cohen-Stratyner, Barbara Naomi. *Biographical Dictionary of Dance.* New York: Schirmer Books, 1982.

Grant, Gail. *Technical Manual and Directory of Classical Ballet.* New York: Dover, 1982.

Koegler, Horst. *The Concise Oxford Dictionary of Ballet.* London: Oxford University Press, 1982.

Steinberg, Cobbett, ed. *The Dance Anthology.* New York: New American Library, 1980.

TECHNIQUE

Bruhn, Erik, and Lillian Moore. *Bournonville and Ballet Technique.* London: Adam & Charles Black, 1961.

Glasstone, Richard. *Better Ballet.* Cranbury, N.J.: A. S. Barnes, 1977.

Hammond, Sandra Noll. *Ballet: Beyond the Basics.* Palo Alto: Mayfield Publishing Co., 1982.

Karsavina, Tamara. *Classical Ballet: The Flow of Movement.* London: Adam & Charles Black, 1962.

Lawson, Joan. *The Principles of Classical Dance.* London: Adam & Charles Black, 1979.

Stuart, Muriel, and Lincoln Kirstein. *The Classic Ballet.* New York: Knopf, 1982.

Vaganova, Agrippina. *Basic Principles of Classical Ballet.* New York: Dover, 1969.

CARE OF THE BODY

Arnheim, Daniel D. *Dance Injuries: Their Prevention and Cure.* St. Louis: Mosby, 1980.

Dunn, Beryl. *Dance! Therapy for Dancers.* London: Heinemann Health Books, 1979.

Featherstone, Donald F. *Dancing Without Danger.* South Brunswick and New York: A. S. Barnes, 1970.

Sparger, Celia. *Anatomy and Ballet.* London: Adam & Charles Black, 1982.

Vincent, L. M. *Competing with the Sylph: Dancers and the Pursuit of the Ideal Body Form.* New York: Andrews & McMeel, 1980.

———. *The Dancer's Book of Health.* Kansas City, Kans.: Andrews & McMeel, 1978.

BALLET PROFESSION

d'Amboise, Christopher. *A Year in the Life of a Dancer.* Garden City, N.Y.: Doubleday, 1982.

Dance Magazine Annual. New York: Danad, published annually.

Glasstone, Richard. *Male Dancing as a Career.* London: Kaye & Ward, 1980.

Jacob, Ellen. *Dancing: A Guide for the Dancer You Can Be.* Reading, Mass.: Addison-Wesley, 1981.

Martins, Peter. *Far from Denmark.* Boston: Little, Brown, 1982.

Mazo, Joseph. *Dance Is a Contact Sport.* New York: Da Capo Press, 1974.

Neal, Wendy, *Ballet Life Behind the Scenes.* New York: Crown, 1982.

Reynolds, Nancy, ed. *The Dance Catalogue.* New York: Harmony Books, 1979.

BALLET VIEWING

Cohen, Selma Jeanne. *Next Week Swan Lake: Reflections on Dance and Dancers.* Middletown, Conn.: Wesleyan University Press, 1982.

Croce, Arlene, *Going to the Dance.* New York: Knopf, 1982.

———. *Afterimages.* New York: Random House, Vintage Books, 1979.

McDonagh, Don. *How to Enjoy the Ballet.* Garden City, N.Y.: Doubleday, Dolphin Books, 1980.

Siegel, Marcia B. *At the Vanishing Point.* New York: Saturday Review Press, 1973.

———. *Watching the Dance Go By.* Boston: Houghton Mifflin, 1977.

Terry, Walter. *I Was There.* New York: Marcel Dekker, 1978.

HISTORY

Anderson, Jack. *Dance.* New York: Newsweek Books, 1979.
Bland, Alexander. *A History of Ballet and Dance.* New York: Praeger, 1976.
Cohen, Selma Jeanne. *Dance as a Theatre Art: Selected Readings in Dance History.* New York: Dodd, Mead, 1974.
Guest, Ivor. *The Dancer's Heritage: A Short History of Ballet.* London: The Dancing Times, 1979.
Kirstein, Lincoln. *Dance: A Short History of Classical Theatrical Dancing.* New York: Dance Horizons, 1977.
Kraus, Richard, and Sarah Alberti Chapman. *History of the Dance in Art and Education.* Englewood Cliffs, N.J.: Prentice-Hall, 1981.

MOSTLY PICTORIAL

Clarke, Mary, and Clement Crisp. *Ballet Art from the Renaissance to the Present.* New York: Potter, 1978.
France, Charles Engell. *Baryshnikov at Work.* New York: Knopf, 1979.
Kahn, Albert E. *Days with Ulanova.* New York: Simon & Schuster, 1962.
Kirstein, Lincoln. *Movement and Metaphor: Four Centuries of Ballet.* New York: Praeger, 1970.
Kochno, Boris. *Diaghilev and the Ballets Russes.* New York: Harper & Row, 1979.
Migel, Parmenia. *Great Ballet Prints of the Romantic Era.* New York: Dover, 1981.
Moore, Lillian. *Images of the Dance.* New York: N.Y. Public Library, 1965.

PERIODICALS

Ballet News (monthly), 1865 Broadway, New York, N.Y. 10023.
Ballet Review (quarterly), 46 Morton Street, New York, N.Y. 10014.
Dance Chronicle (quarterly), P.O. Box 1105, Church Street Station, New York, N.Y. 10249.
Dance Magazine (monthly), P.O. Box 960, Farmingdale, N.Y. 11737.

TECHNICAL TERMS INDEX

Page numbers refer to major explanations of technical terms. Italicized numbers refer to illustrations. Additional entries for these terms are given in the General Index.

GENERAL INDEX

Italicized numbers refer to illustrations.